On The Trail Of Liberation

A Recounting of
Precious Moments with Amma

On the Trail of Liberation
Vol. 5

A Recounting of Precious Moments with Amma

Edited by Br. Madhavamrita Chaitanya

Published by:
Mata Amritanandamayi Center
P.O. Box 613
San Ramon, CA 94583-0613, USA

In India:
www.amritapuri.org
inform@amritapuri.org

In Europe:
www.amma-europe.org

In US:
www.amma.org

On The Trail Of Liberation

A Recounting of Precious Moments with Amma

Edited by Br. Madhavamrita Chaitanya

Mata Amritanandamayi Center,
San Ramon, California, USA

Contents

Preface

The book you are holding is yet another compilation of *satsaṅgs*, discourses on spiritual topics, that monastics from the Amṛtapuri Āśram gave in Amma's sacred presence.

There are some who would object to applying the label 'satsaṅg' to the talks given by the monastics. They point out that 'satsaṅg' literally means 'companionship with Truth;' for this reason, only talks by *mahātmās* (spiritually illumined souls) like Amma, who embody the Truth, can be called satsaṅgs. All other talks on transpersonal topics may respectfully be termed 'spiritual discourses.'

But don't we use a broad spectrum of words loosely? For example, we might say we are meditating. Naysayers would contend that meditation is a noun, not a verb. It is a state of stillness, of oneness with the object of meditation, whereas what most of us do in the name of meditation is to *practice* stilling the mind. Amma gives another example. Suppose we put some water to boil so that we can make tea. If someone were to ask us what we were doing, we would say, "Making tea." It's not a dishonest or disingenuous answer, but one that indicates what we *intend* to do.

Likewise, we can justify calling these talks satsaṅgs. They are meant to take both speaker and listener closer to the Truth. Because they were given in the presence of someone who embodies the Truth, they have the same ring of seriousness as oaths taken in the presence of a judge. The *intent* is to speak the truth; the caveat being, it is the truth as they understand or see it. Amma has, with characteristic generosity, called these talks satsaṅgs.

What is significant is that almost everything the speakers said were shaped and influenced by Amma, her teachings and their experiences with her. Even when they discuss verses from the *Bhagavad Gītā*, they do so in the light of Amma's sublime wisdom. In that sense, the talks are satsaṅgs because they point inevitably to Amma, the personification of Truth.

Even if we are in Amma's physical presence, what matters primarily is whether our mind is *present*. Thereafter, we must contemplate or reflect on what she says or does. Our understanding is always commensurate with our level of maturity. We hope that the satsaṅgs in this compilation will deepen your understanding of spiritual principles and heighten the light of awareness. If they do, you will have moved closer to the Truth.

Br. Mādhavāmṛta Caitanya

Necessity of a Guru

A Message from Amma

Children, the scriptures say that God is within us, and that He is not separate from us. If so, some people might wonder why a Guru is necessary. God is within us, but to realize this, we must rely on a Guru to eliminate the ego in us. Only someone who is awake can awaken someone who is in deep sleep. To light a wick, we need the flame from another burning wick. Similarly, in order to realize God within us, we need the help of a spiritually enlightened master.

If we dig for a well in certain places, we will never be able to find water no matter how deep we dig. But if we dig near a river, we will hit water after just a bit of digging. Likewise, the disciple's noble qualities and talents will soon manifest in the Guru's presence.

The Guru will create situations to help the disciple get rid of his laziness, overcome his *vāsanās* (latent tendencies), and enable him to realize the Truth. Once, a Guru and his disciple were returning to their āśram after a pilgrimage. Half way through the journey, the disciple said, "O Guru, I cannot take even one step further! Let me rest under this banyan tree for a while." The master insisted that they continue, but the disciple refused. The master continued his journey alone. He saw some people working in a field by the roadside. Their children were playing nearby. A baby was fast asleep on the ground. Without their noticing, the Guru picked up the baby and placed it next to his disciple, who was sleeping under the tree. The Guru then hid himself.

When the workers noticed that the baby was missing, there was chaos! They started running hither and thither in search of the baby. Hearing the commotion, the disciple woke up. The workers angrily asked him, "Did you steal our baby?" and were about to pounce on him. The disciple jumped up and ran for life, soon reaching the āśram. The Guru walked at a leisurely pace, and when he reached the āśram, he found the disciple sleeping in exhaustion. The Guru asked him, "You said that you couldn't take even one more step. But you reached the āśram before me." When the disciple is reluctant to obey the Guru's words, he will do anything it takes to bring him back to the right path.

Today, we are slaves to our mind and sense organs. But if we obey the Guru's instructions, we will be free from this slavery forever.

1

The True Dharma of Life

Swāmī Vivēkāmṛtānanda Puri

A year after I joined the āśram, Amma asked me, "Son, can you go out and give *satsaṅgs* (discourses on a spiritual topic)?"

The question was unexpected. Even though I did not know what to say, the answer that came to mind was, "If it's Amma's will." When her power acts through me, I will surely be able to do anything. How can anyone do anything otherwise? Amma often says, "Even to close our mouth after yawning, we need God's grace."

Once, a devotee was singing bhajans at Amma's Kozhikode branch āśram. When she finished singing, her mouth remained open. She could not close it, no matter how much she tried. She was taken to a hospital. The doctors there could not close her mouth either and decided she needed surgery. She was taken to the Kozhikode Medical College, where the doctors succeeded in closing her mouth without surgery.

The power that moves the universal body also moves the individual body. That formless power has assumed a form: Amma's. The scriptures, which are the words of people who have experienced God, describe that power as *nitya* (eternal), *śuddha* (pure), *mukta* (liberated) and *buddha* (enlightened). How can we give a satsaṅg if all we do is borrow words from others? With this doubt, I asked Amma, "Isn't it only when one has experienced God that one is qualified to give a satsaṅg?"

Amma replied, "Son, you're doing it only because Amma told you, right? Then see it as a spiritual practice."

Preparing a satsaṅg involves meditation and contemplation. Just as one who plucks flowers for offering to God enjoys their fragrance first, the one who prepares the satsaṅg is benefited before the audience hears it. Contemplation encourages us to look within. In that sense, it is like a mirror that helps us see our inner impurities. Any talk we give ought to be based only on how we have applied the knowledge we have acquired in our personal lives. We must honor Amma's words and turn a satsaṅg into a means to purify ourselves.

The main scriptures in Sanātana Dharma — the Vēdas, Itihāsas and Purāṇas — describe the four *puruṣārthas* or main goals of human life: namely *dharma* (duties), *artha* (wealth), *kāma* (desires) and *mōkṣa* (liberation). The Itihāsas — the *Rāmāyaṇa* and *Mahābhārata* — in particular have had a profound impact on Indian culture. The *Rāmāyaṇa* is an epic biography of about Lord Rāma. The author of the *Rāmāyaṇa* considered the Lord the ideal man.

Once, Sage Nārada visited the hermitage of Sage Vālmīki, who received him in the traditional way. During their conversation, Vālmīki asked Nārada:

> *ko nvasmin sāmpratam lōkē guṇavān kaśca vīryavān*
> *dharmajñaśca kṛtajñaśca satyavākyō dṛḍhavrataḥ*
> Who in the world today is virtuous and valorous, righteous and grateful, honest and of firm resolve? (Bāla Kāṇḍa, 1.1.2)

When Nārada heard this question, he saw the form of Lord Rāma in his mind. He started to recount the story of Lord Rāma to Vālmīki. This is how the *Rāmāyaṇa* begins. The epic has inspired generations to follow the path of dharma (righteous living) for thousands of years. Historians say that the events described in the *Rāmāyaṇa* occurred 7,000 years ago. Though many centuries have passed since then, Lord Rāma's life continues to inspire many people today.

"... virtuous and valorous, righteous and grateful, honest and of firm resolve." We can see one or two of the qualities mentioned in other characters in the *Rāmāyaṇa*. But all of them find their home in Rāma. Such is his glory.

According to an ancient proverb, '*yathā rājā tathā prajā*'—'As is the king, so are the subjects.' If the king turns his back on truth and dharma, then who can or will correct him? If a king breaks his vows, his subjects may follow suit.

At the time of his marriage to Kaikēyī, Daśaratha promised her that he would crown her son as king. But as he was too attached to Rāma, his eldest son, he tried to renege on his promise. When Sage Viśwāmitra sought permission to take Rāma and Lakṣmaṇa to the forest so that they could protect the *yajñas* (fire sacrifices), the king did not accede to the request. It was only after Sage Vasiṣṭha intervened that Daśaratha relented.

When Rāma was about to be crowned, Kaikēyī demanded that Daśaratha honors his promise to her. This demand caused the king to sink deep into sorrow. But Śrī Rāma vowed to uphold his father's promise. Even his mother, Kausalyā, proved to be too attached, and tried to prevent Rāma from going to the forest. She said, "If you're going to the forest to honor your father's words, heed your mother, who is telling you not to go. The scriptures declare that a mother's words are more important than a father's. So, shouldn't you obey your mother?"

Śrī Rāma answered, "Mother, your words are inspired by attachment to me and not righteousness."

After Rāvaṇa died, Vibhīṣaṇa expressed contempt for his corpse. But Rāma insisted that Rāvaṇa be honored with a royal cremation. He reminded Vibhīṣaṇa to condemn the unrighteous acts of a person and not the person.

Sugrīva lost his kingdom and his wife because of his brother Vāli, whom Rāma killed as punishment for his adharmic deeds. As he lay dying, Vāli said that Rāma's killing was unrighteous. But after hearing Rāma's justification, Vāli accepted the death sentence. It was not Rāma who killed Vāli but the inviolable law of dharma acting through Rāma. The universal law of dharma is expressed in the following saying:

> *dharma ēva hatō hanti dharmō rakṣati rakṣitaḥ*
> One who annihilates dharma gets annihilated by dharma. One who protects dharma is in turn protected by dharma.

In killing Rāvaṇa, Rāma was only fulfilling his *rājadharma* (kingly duties). The dharma of a king is to ensure the safety of his subjects and to safeguard his kingdom and culture. His duties encompass the governance, protection and uplifting of his subjects.

After rescuing Sītā, Rāma insisted that Sītā follow *pativrata dharma* (wifely duties). But when Rāma learned that his subjects wondered if Sītā's chastity had been compromised during her stay in Lanka, Rāma sacrificed his love for Sītā. Rāma loved dharma more than anyone. He was prepared to make any sacrifice to uphold dharma. This is the greatness of Lord Rāma.

But this is very difficult for ordinary people to accept. That's why people criticize Rāma, saying things like, "If I were in Rāma's place, I wouldn't have sacrificed Sītā." But this is the attitude of one who is enslaved by sensual pleasures and attachments. At first, sacrificing our pleasures might seem too difficult. Sacrifice is difficult in the beginning, but in the end, it gives joy. Such is the way of sacrifice.

Jābāli, an atheist, told Rāma, "What's the point of fulfilling the promise of your dead father? All obligations ended with his death. You should take over the kingdom, which is yours by right. What's the use of offering oblations to the departed? Those who do so are wasting rice. How can the rice intended for the departed reach them? Exiling yourself to fulfill your father's pledge does not serve any purpose. Therefore, return to Ayodhya and rule as king!"

After listening to him patiently, Rāma said, "O Jābāli, what you're saying seems to be true, but it's not. It seems to be dharmic, but it's not. The only truth is God. There is no goal above truth. *Hōmas* (fire ceremonies), *dāna* (charity), *yajña* (ritual oblations), *tapas* (austerity) and the Vēdas (scripture) are based on Truth. Therefore, everyone should adhere to the truth."

Rāma was committed to truth and dharma. *Mahātmās* (spiritually illumined souls) are ready to sacrifice anything for dharma. This is India's greatest ideal as well. It is one of the main principles guiding her:

> *tyajēd-ēkam kulasyārthē grāmasyārthē kulam tyajēt*
> *grāmam janapadasyārthē ātmārthē pṛthivīm tyajēt*

Sacrifice one member for the sake of the family. Give up
a family for the sake of a village.
Sacrifice a village for the benefit of the country, and
give up the earth for the sake of the Self.

It is not easy to follow the path of righteousness while living in this world. If someone reminds us about moral values, we might tell them, "Those values were inscribed in ancient scriptures. Who can follow them now?" Is it possible to live in accordance with moral values?

Throughout the ages, there have always been spiritual masters, who follow dharma, irrespective of the prevailing lifestyles of the times. They are spiritual powerhouses that can influence millions of people and lead them on the path of dharma. That is why, in the *Bhagavad Gītā*, Lord Kṛṣṇa says:

yadyad ācarati śrēṣṭhas-tattad ēvētarō janaḥ
sa yat pramāṇam kurutē lōkas-tad anuvartatē
Whatever actions great people do, the masses will
emulate.
The world will strive to rise up to the standards they
set. (3.21)

We begin the inner journey towards perfection when we meet a mahātmā, established in perfection. This is the meaning and essence of the word 'Rāmāyaṇa.' It does not mean only 'Rāma's journey' but also our journey to attain the Rāma principle, which is the principle of perfection.

All of us who have reached Amma have knowingly or unknowingly been searching for this perfection. Anyone who yearns for this ideal will be attracted to Amma.

Before I heard about Amma, I read a book my mother had: *The Gospel of Sri Ramakrishna*. It awakened the spiritual quest lying dormant inside me. I felt that life would be meaningful only if I followed the path of spirituality. I saw my *vāsanās* (latent tendencies) as hindrances to my spiritual life. I knew I needed a Guru's disciplining to move forward in this path.

I decided to spend the rest of my life in the Sri Ramakrishna Math in Thrissur. I met Swāmī Śakrānanda, then the President of the Math, who was pleased with my decision. When he learned that I was from Alappuzha, he asked me to meet Muraleedhara Menon, a professor at a college there. He said that the professor had a good relationship with the Math.

The next day, I went to the professor's house. I told him about my desire to join the āśram and recounted my conversation with Śakrānanda Swāmījī. I also told him that I was looking for a Guru like Śrī Rāmakṛṣṇa. When he heard that, the professor spoke to me about Amma. I asked him what it was about Amma that reminded him of Śrī Rāmakṛṣṇa. His reply struck me with wonder:

> Amma is a girl who is intoxicated with love for God. She sings divine songs and dances. At other times, she forgets the world and becomes engrossed in meditation. She eats only if somebody forcefully feeds her. She will lie down in dirty water and completely forget herself.

When he narrated this, I recalled how Śrī Rāmakṛṣṇa would weep like a child on the banks of the Ganges for a glimpse of Kālī, the Divine Mother. Once, he even took Kālī's sword from the shrine and tried to chop his head off! Kālī appeared before him, and he completely forgot the universe.

I felt that I had found the answer to my search. I saw Amma's perfection in her life of sacrifice. I was reminded of Narendra (Swāmī Vivēkānanda), who heard about the priest of Dakshineswar from his British professor during his college days in Kolkata. Narendra went to meet him and asked. "Have you seen God?"

"Child, I see God clearer than I see you," replied Śrī Rāmakṛṣṇa.

This was the turning point in my life. I went to Vallikavu to meet Amma. She was giving darśan. I expressed my desire to stay in the āśram with her. Amma said, "Son, for the time being, come and go. Amma will tell you later when you can stay permanently in the āśram."

I was feeling reluctant to call her 'Amma' as the term is used only with our mother or an elderly woman. So, when Amma whispered into my ear, "Son," I just mumbled "Umm..."

Amma repeated, "Son." I mumbled again. But after she called me son for the third time, I instinctively answered, "Amma!" There was a special sweetness to Amma's voice when she called me son. I felt it came from the depth of her soul. She then spoke to me about the need to work for the ideals of dharma.

I returned home happily. I started coming to the āśram frequently in the hope that Amma would permit me to stay. I had to wait for five more years to get Amma's permission to stay permanently in the āśram.

The qualities that attracted so many people to Śrī Rāma and Śrī Kṛṣṇa are the same qualities that are manifest in Amma. Multitudes are attracted to her because of these qualities.

For someone who wishes to see God as king, Lord Rāma is ideal. In the *Dwāpara Yuga,*[1] Lord Kṛṣṇa removed unrighteous kings from their thrones and installed righteous kings. We no longer revere kings as we did in ancient times. So, if God were to come as a king, nobody would be attracted to him. Therefore, in the present age, God has manifested in the form of a universal mother. Who else but Amma can hold people's hands and uplift them?

In Amma, we can see the perfection of the Mā-Ōm meditation. 'Mā' means love and 'Ōm' means light. Amma combines the light of self-knowledge and the love of universal motherhood. In 'Amma,' 'Am' means 'letter' or 'self-knowledge.' The Self is an indestructible essence.

In 'Rāma,' 'Ra' means light and 'Mā' means love. Thus, we can see how the spiritual principles in Rāma and motherhood are the same.

The meaning of both 'Amma' and 'Rāma' denotes this common principle.

People were not drawn to Lord Rāma because of his wondrous deeds, but because he practiced the supreme ideals throughout his life. Temptations and threats could not shake his determination. When Sugrīva asked Rāma to demonstrate his strength, the Lord kicked the giant skeleton of Dundubhi, a buffalo demon, with his toe. He then pierced seven giant palm

---

1 *One of the four* yugas *(epochs), that, according to the Hindu worldview, make up one cycle of creation, from origin to dissolution. The first is* Kṛta Yuga, *during which dharma reigns in society. Each succeeding age sees the progressive decline of dharma. The second age is known as* Trēta Yuga, *the third is* Dwāpara Yuga, *and the fourth and present epoch is known as* Kali Yuga.

trees with a single arrow. His arrows pierced mountaintops and the earth itself.

Lord Kṛṣṇa revealed his superhuman might by lifting the Gōvardhana Mountain to shelter the villagers from the wrath of Indra, the god of rains. But Amma says that Kṛṣṇa's real miracle was awakening devotion in the *gōpīs* (milkmaids) of Vṛndāvan. God always glorifies his devotees.

What attracted the gōpīs to Lord Kṛṣṇa? They saw in him the ideals of omnipresence, omniscience and omnipotence. People are attracted for the same reasons to Amma, like iron filings to a magnet.

Mahātmās are like a flame that stands unwavering in a cyclone. Established in truth and righteousness, they march ahead, illuminating the path to liberation. Without their guiding light, we would be in darkness. What paves the path to the truth and righteousness is sacrifice. Many are ready to tread along the razor's edge because of their love for Amma. Her motherly assurance — "Amma will hold your hands and guide you. Amma will break the shackles constraining you" — is our inspiration.

The existence of this universe is predicated on dharma. So, whenever there is a decline in dharma, God will incarnate to restore it.

In the *Mahābhārata*, Sage Vyāsa says, *"Dharmasya tattwam nihitam guhāyām"* — "The principles of dharma are difficult to understand and follow." How can we learn to differentiate between dharma and adharma? *"Mahājanō yēna gataḥ sa panthāḥ"* — "One must follow in the footsteps of saints."

If we look at Amma's life, we will see that all her actions are aimed at sustaining dharma. She sacrifices everything to uphold the *Sanātana Dharma* (eternal principles). Through example,

Amma shows us how to love people unconditionally. There are countless instances of people who were once antagonistic to Amma but whom she welcomed lovingly and who are now dedicated to Amma and her mission.

Amma consecrated Brahmasthānam temples and educated people about the principles behind idol worship. She also started the Amrita Vidyalayam schools and Amrita Vishwa Vidyapeetham (university) to promote value-based education. She stresses the importance of combining science and spirituality. Amma has also spearheaded many initiatives in the agricultural, medical, environmental and public health sectors over the past four decades.

In January 2020, Amma concluded the annual Brahmasthānam Temple festival in Kozhikode by giving her children a gift—a few lines written in her own handwriting: "Life is very short. In this short span of time, we must make ourselves and others happy. It is by giving love that..."

She did not complete the sentence. It was as if Amma wanted us to complete it according to our own understanding. I felt the sentence could be ended like this: "It is by giving love that we can enjoy the beauty of life."

Through this small message, Amma is conveying the dharma of human life: to live with true love.

2

Light of Her Grace

Swāmī Śāntāmṛtānanda Puri

There are many definitions of the word *'yōga,'* one of which is 'the application of spirituality in one's life.' The first chapter of the *Bhagavad Gītā* is called *'Arjuna Viṣāda Yōgaḥ'*—'The Yōga of Arjuna's Despondency.' In other words, despondency is supposed to be a kind of yōga. If you were to open a yōga studio in a place like New York, Paris or Munich, and put up a big sign that read, 'Despondency Yōga,' how many students do you think would come? Probably none. But if you put up a sign that read, 'Yōga that will Turn your Dejection into Happiness,' the whole city would sign up. This is precisely what Amma does for us: She teaches us how to convert our sorrow into happiness, which is true yōga. This is also a common theme in the story about how each one of us came to Amma.

I found myself here in Amṛtapuri about 30 years ago, just six months after meeting Amma for the first time. Looking back, I ask myself, "How did I get here?" For that matter, how did all of us get here? The mere fact of being one of the 38 million people who have met Amma puts us in the 99.5th percentile of the 7.8 billion people in the world.

How can we account for this rare blessing we have all received? There can only be two answers: either the cause comes from us or it comes from something other than us.

Perhaps it is our good karma from past lives. Perhaps we did so many good deeds over many lifetimes that we received this good fortune. This conclusion is certainly pleasing to the ego!

But no matter how many good deeds we have done, they are still finite whereas meeting Amma is an infinite gift that no combination of good deeds could have produced. Some scriptural texts refer to rituals or austerities that can fulfill worldly desires, even that of attaining the status of Indra, the chief of the gods. But even the gods in heaven have not been blessed to come under the guidance of the Divine Mother whereas we have. The only factor that can explain the immeasurable blessing of having Amma in our lives is her own infinite grace. The Guru's grace is that causeless cause, to which we can attribute all the mysteries and miracles that take place around Amma.

Amma once said, "Nothing is possible without grace. Whether in this birth, in the previous birth, or in the births yet to come, one cannot acquire a spiritual disposition without the Guru's grace. If you have any spiritual disposition inherited from the previous birth, that was also gained through the Guru's grace."

This means that the Guru makes unqualified people worthy of being in the Guru's presence. There are so many stories of angry and spiteful people, drug addicts and drug dealers, convicted felons, those who exploited others to increase their own wealth, and so on, who reached Amma. None of them fit the scriptural description of one who is eligible to become a devotee or disciple. Nonetheless, they did, by Amma's grace.

Once, during darśan in New York City, a man tried to ask Amma a question during darśan. But as it was too busy, she told him to come to her side to ask his question. He told me, "Tomorrow in court, the judge will pass the verdict in my case. Please ask Amma to pray for me."

I asked him, "Just in case Amma asks, what's the case about?"

"Drug smuggling. By the way, I'm guilty."

Trying to conceal any sign of a reaction, I turned back to Amma to convey the message. But what I saw made me freeze. A uniformed officer from the New York Police Department was about to receive a hug from Amma. After he had darśan, I conveyed the drug smuggler's request to Amma. She rubbed his chest and told him to be courageous and to surrender everything to God. For a long time, he sat beside Amma, weeping what seemed like tears of bitter remorse. Finally, as he got up to leave, he told me, "I don't know what I would do if I didn't have Amma in my life. I probably would have ended my life before the judge's verdict. But now I'm at peace, because I know everything is in her hands. Whatever happens is for the best."

Later, I found out that he was given a light sentence. Afterwards, he cleaned up his act and is now helping drug addicts reform themselves. He went from being part of the problem to becoming a role model inspiring others to rid themselves of their addictions. This dramatic transformation came about only by Amma's grace!

If Amma can help such an extreme case, surely, she can help anyone. I, too, did not fulfill a single precondition to receive the blessing of meeting Amma. My horoscope certainly does not indicate I was a great yōgī or pious devotee in a recent birth. I was born into a typical American family. We weren't vegetarians, didn't go to church, watched TV, and enjoyed the pleasures of the world without seeking something higher in life. As teenagers, my friends and I did more naughty things than I care to remember! As a young adult, I was restless, quick to anger, and extremely arrogant.

During the final year of my undergraduate studies, my dream was to join the military and become a helicopter pilot. Right after graduation, I was accepted into officer candidate school, which made me even more arrogant. But soon after I was accepted, something happened that made me reconsider my decision, and this changed the entire course of my life. That 'something' was Amma.

The first question I ever asked Amma was, "Should I join the military or go to law school?"

Amma looked at me with a loving, all-knowing expression, and said, "Son, whatever you do, wherever you go, Amma is always with you." Then she added, "But don't forget the importance of education."

I thought, "Ah! She wants me to go to law school!" But obviously, that did not happen.

It was only years later that I understood the depth of Amma's words. After I asked her that question, through various circumstances, I spent two years working for the government in rural Japan. I also did a tiny bit of *sēvā* (selfless service) for Amma but felt guilty that I could not do more.

One day during my second visit to Amṛtapuri in 1992, I was sitting outside the old darśan hut, waiting for Amma to come out, so that I could catch a glimpse of her as she returned to her room. There were only about five or six of us there. When Amma came out, I lowered my head and joined my palms prayerfully.

Amma grabbed my hands, pulled me closer, and started telling the others something about me in Malayāḷam. She went on and on. I was getting curious. Finally, someone translated. Amma had described in detail all the things that I had done in Japan. I had never mentioned a word of it to Amma or anyone else in the āśram. Not only that, she even said that I did all the things that I wished I had done but did not because of laziness or a lack of commitment.

At that time, I understood that Amma doesn't speak lightly. Those words, "Amma is always with you, wherever you go," were not mere encouragement. They were and forever remain the reality. As she sings in *'Ōmkāra Divya Poruḷē,'* "You are the 'I' in me and I am the 'you' in you. The feeling of difference is caused by the blindness of ignorance. In truth, nothing is separate."

Such unforgettable experiences can only be attributed to her grace. I'm sure each person can share the magical and blissful feeling that filled them after meeting Amma for the first time. Many of our most precious memories are from that period of our life. Due to our innocence, our mind becomes like a clean slate, upon which Amma can freely script a new destiny for us. Amma once said, "Self-effort is limited; Grace is unlimited. The limited human effort can take you only so far. From that point, it is the vehicle of the Guru's grace that carries you to the goal. Do your *sādhana* (spiritual practices) sincerely, with an attitude of self-surrender and love. Then patiently wait for grace to come."

In my case, Amma's grace usually came in the form of her physical presence during her annual visit to Japan. There were few people to coordinate her programs in the early 90s, which meant that I got to be with Amma all day every day while trying to help. But as I was inexperienced then, I had no idea what I was doing, and ended up making a mess of everything! Though Amma says that the disciple should wait patiently, in my case, it was the Guru who waited patiently!

The 1993 Tokyo program was a perfect example. On the morning of the first day, owing to a lack of experience, I was frantic and disoriented. As a result, even arranging the transportation was a challenge for me. Amma waited patiently in the lobby of the accommodation for her car to arrive. After a long wait, the car finally came and Amma could leave. What a relief!

But when I turned around, I saw four swāmīs standing before me, anxious expressions on their faces; I had totally forgotten to arrange a car for them! As we were already late for the program, I ran out and flagged a taxi for them. As I watched the swāmīs' car drive off, I heaved a sigh of relief, knowing that everyone was now on their way to the venue... everyone except me!

I panicked. I had to be there to lead the guided meditation at the beginning! I looked, hoping to flag down another taxi, but at that moment, every single taxi in Tokyo seemed to have disappeared. With no time to waste, I started running to the venue, which was more than 2 kilometers (1.5 miles) away. I couldn't run very fast as I was wearing Indian slippers. I removed them and ran barefoot. Then it started to rain. The whole time, I was thinking, "Oh no, Amma's going to be angry! She will never forgive me!"

Finally, I reached the hall, soaking wet. The program venue was on the fifth floor and there was a long line of elderly people in front of the elevator. I decided to sprint up the stairs as quickly as possible. As I was 24 years old then, that wasn't a problem. But when I reached the hall, I was totally out of breath.

I was 20 minutes late and expected to see an angry Amma as I entered the hall. But what did I see? Amma was playing with the small children in the front of the hall. In those 20 minutes, she had become their best friend and won over the hearts of their parents. I thought to myself, "Wow, every second is so precious for Amma!"

I sat down next to Amma to lead the meditation, but after all that running, I was panting hard! I was also so stressed out that instead of waiting to catch my breath, I just started: "Close your eyes *(pant, pant)...* breathe slowly, but naturally *(pant, pant).* Feel fully relaxed.... *(pant, pant)*" Everybody must have wondered, "What is wrong with this guy?" Understanding my mental condition, Amma reached over and stroked my arm to calm me down. I looked at her and saw perfect peace in her eyes. She wasn't mad at all, not even the slightest bit disturbed.

Just that one glance from Amma was the grace I needed. My breathing slowed down immediately. All my stress and worries disappeared, and I could conduct the meditation without any problem.

As Amma says, our effort is always finite—and sometimes full of mistakes! It is the Guru's grace that compensates for all our shortcomings.

The following day, the topic of my original name came up. My parents had named me Brandon. As this name is unfamiliar in India, one of the swāmīs pronounced it for Amma a few times. Suddenly, Amma burst into laughter, saying "*Bhrāntan!*"—"Crazy man!" After the previous day's escapades, I thoroughly deserved that new nickname.

Since then, almost three decades have passed and while I have certainly learned a lot from Amma over the years, I sometimes yearn to regain the original feeling I had at that time. When we first meet Amma, we don't know anything and are aware of our ignorance. This humility draws grace. Amma says, "When the disciple feels, 'I am nothing,' the Guru's grace will unknowingly flow to him." So, in one sense, Amma is patiently waiting for us to become 'nothing,' because that is when we will yearn for her grace and be worthy of it, too.

Amma's brother, Satheesh, tells a touching story. Once, when Amma was about 16 years old, he found her sitting by the backwaters. Her eyes were brimming with tears. At first, he thought someone might have scolded or beaten her. He asked Amma, "Why these tears?"

Amma looked at him and said, "Son, I can feel the sorrows of the world. I can hear the cries of suffering humanity and I know how to remove their sorrow, but, alas, nobody wants the solution. These tears are for humanity." This is Amma's only sorrow—our sleep of ignorance. It is far more painful for her than for us because we are oblivious to the bliss of the Self that we are missing.

What can we do now to invoke her grace? Amma has already told us: "Selfless service and total dedication are the two things that make one worthy of the Guru's grace. The goal of the spiritual path is to understand the suffering of the sick and the poor, and to lead a life of selfless service to them. A seeker's every breath should be one of compassion for the suffering. Your thought should be, 'I am not doing sādhana for my own selfish goals but for the world.'... Renunciation is the readiness to offer to the world the strength gained through sādhana. That is a true seeker's only aim."

Please note that Amma doesn't talk about who is physically closer to her or far away; she doesn't mention where you were born, what language you speak, or how good you are in singing or doing pūjā . All she wants to see is compassion growing in our heart.

Amma reassures us also. She says, "As we walk on the spiritual path, there is a light guiding us. That light is the Guru's grace. The Guru walks in front, shedding light on the path, as she carefully leads us... The light of her grace helps us to see and overcome the obstacles, until we reach the ultimate goal."

3

A Child's Heart

Swāminī Śivapriyāmṛta Prāṇā

Once, while speaking on how Arjuna's despondency became *yōga* (a path to God), Swāmī Amṛtaswarūpānanda (Swāmījī) offered a response that I felt was unique. He said that when Arjuna realized that his opponents were relatives and friends, he became mentally paralyzed. He dropped his bow and tried to withdraw from the war. His inability to act arose because he was confused. When such confusion arises, we can either retreat from action or surrender to the situation. Surrender leads to inner clarity. Until then, we will remain confused. Confusion leads to tension, which will not allow the light of discernment to brighten our mind. But with surrender, we can unburden ourselves mentally.

Arjuna's inner conflict became so unbearable that he wanted to quit the battle. In utter hopelessness, he surrendered to the Lord and pleaded to be saved from his confusion. Arjuna became like a child, thus awakening maternal love in the Lord, who became ready to express the milk of divine wisdom.

Just as the Lord's motherhood was stirred when Arjuna's child-like heart was roused, the Guru in Kṛṣṇa manifested itself when Arjuna surrendered to him with the attitude of a true disciple. The Guru-disciple relationship is similar to the bond between mother and child.

Amma often reminds us about the importance of a child-like heart in spirituality. The very word 'child' generates joy and enthusiasm because a child's heart is pure. His innocence and purity make him receptive. A seeker is also expected to go beyond likes and dislikes and keep an open mind. This attitude of acceptance enables him to welcome every situation. In this way, we can make each day festive, as children do. This is what Amma wants for us, too.

A young child's mind is filled only with thoughts of its mother — her look, touch, voice and scent. She is his sole support and strength. The disciple who has surrendered to the Guru becomes like a child. For him, the Guru is everything. To illustrate, Amma narrates the story of two children who went to swim in a pool. One of them dived into the water fearlessly, but the other shrank back in fear. Seeing this, an onlooker asked the child who was frolicking in the pool, "Aren't you scared?"

"No," he said. "My mum's here to take care of me!"

Such a firm and abiding faith in the Guru is essential for spiritual seekers, for whom the Guru must become everything.

For me, after meeting Amma, it became difficult to stay away from her. Earlier, I had been attached to my mother, Radhamma. I also enjoyed an abundance of material pleasures as well as love from the rest of my family. Yet, after meeting Amma, I was able to forgo all those readily and live away from them. The only explanation for this is the timeless bond between Amma and me.

Before joining the āśram, I would weep intensely at the end of each visit to Amṛtapuri, when I had to go back home. Once, Amma told me during darśan that she was aware of my grief.

She said that my pain was like that of an unripe mango that had been plucked. What she meant was that it was painful for both the mango and the tree; in other words, for both mother and daughter.

At the beginning, a seeker is a toddler on the spiritual path. Just as a child manages to stand up with the help of his mother, who helps him take his first baby steps, the Guru holds the disciple by hand and leads him gradually to the goal. The toddler walks falteringly but has the faith that his mother is ever ready to catch him if he falls.

Amma is both the guide and the goal. Owing to our intense eagerness to be with her, we strive to move ahead somehow. We might stumble and fall, but we must get up and continue with enthusiasm and the faith that Amma is always with us.

The child has another wonderful quality — he is able to forget. When his mother scolds him, he cries out and clings to her even more firmly. A little later, when his mother showers her love, he forgets the scolding in a moment.

The late Bri. Bhāvāmṛtājī was like this. Amma told her off sharply on many occasions for not giving darśan tokens to devotees. Upset, Bhāvāmṛtājī would rush to her room and cry. Some time later, when told that Amma was calling her, she would run at once to Amma. We would then see her talking and laughing with Amma!

The Guru tests disciples in unexpected ways. Under all circumstances, the disciple must try to maintain an attitude of surrender. We must have the firm conviction that the Guru is our only refuge. Amma has said that before she tests us, she prays that we succeed.

Suppose someone is new to his job. If he makes a mistake and admits it, his superiors will appreciate his honesty and help him deal with the issues to prevent such mistakes from happening again. Instead, if he fails to own up to his mistake, he might lose his job when the mistake is discovered. Similarly, we must be honest and open to the Guru. Only then can we draw her grace and overcome our weaknesses.

How can we awaken the child's heart within? We must delve deep within, as innocence and purity arise in a still mind. To still the mind, we must follow the Guru's instructions and be steadfast in spiritual practice. Obedience is the foundation of discipleship. If a mother's word is final for her child, how much more sacred are the words of a Guru! Obedience will always protect the disciple and take him to his final goal, as illustrated in the following story.

There was once a *Gurukula*[2] with many disciples. The Guru assigned *sēvā* (selfless service) to each one. Most of the sēvā was in and around the āśram, but one disciple had to go into a forest to collect firewood. He would leave early, while it was still dark, and return only after sunset. The forest was full of thorny bushes and wildlife. He would often get pricked by thorns and bleed as a result, but he never minded it. He did his duty, seeing his Guru's words as a divine commandment.

The Guru would go to bed very late at night. Curious about this, his wife decided to find out why.

One night, as always, the disciple returned from the forest with a huge bundle of firewood. After stowing it away, he went

---

2 Literally, the clan (kula) of the preceptor (Guru). A traditional school where students stay with their Guru for the entire duration of their scriptural studies.

to sit in front of the Guru's hut and there meditated for some time. He then lay down. He had no thoughts of his bodily injuries or physical pain, only of his sēvā the next day, and with these thoughts, he fell asleep. The Guru then came to sit near him. Tears of compassion flowed from his eyes to the disciple's body, healing the injuries.

The next morning, the disciple woke up early and, with his usual enthusiasm, set off for the forest, oblivious to the healing of his injuries. In time, by the Guru's grace, the light of *ātma-jñāna* (Self-knowledge) dawned in his heart.

Similarly, many of Amma's devotees have spoken of how they go to bed with physical or mental pain or in a state of tension but wake up refreshed the next morning. This is because Amma comes to them at night to lull them to sleep. She, too, sheds tears of commiseration and showers her compassion on us, thus restoring and recharging us.

The compassion and commiseration that the Divine has for us is reflected in a bhajan that Amma sings:

> *oru pōḷa kaṇṇaṭaccīṭilla mādhavan*
> *karayātirikkilla nammē ōrttu*
> Mādhava (Lord Kṛṣṇa) would not have slept even a wink. He must have been crying, thinking of us. (from '*Karuṇārdra-mānasan*')

Amma has no personal time. She lives each moment for her children. After a long day spent giving darśan, she spends hours reading letters from her children all over the world. Every breath of her life is dedicated to her children and their welfare. We can never repay her, but we can try to cultivate obedience to her.

After completing my undergraduate degree, I wanted to study computer science. I thought of enrolling in a good institute in Kochi. My mother was not keen on this but said that she would consent if Amma permitted. When I told Amma about my desire to study computer science, even before I could tell her about my plan to go to Kochi, she said, "We're starting a computer institute here. Apply at once." Thus, unbeknown to me, Amma opened a door to the spiritual life.

The computer institute was started in 1990, and I was the first student to be admitted! The āśram started a hostel for students. There were strict rules. For health reasons, we were not encouraged to buy food from outside.

One day, I bought a slice of cake from a bakery in Vallikavu. When I returned to the āśram, I heard that Amma was in the kitchen. I went there at once but could not get near her because of the crowd. But I heard Amma saying, "Which computer student ate food from the shop?"

Amma must have known I was present! Using this as an excuse, I pushed my way through the crowd, saying that Amma was calling me. When I reached her, I said, "Amma, it was me!" Amma rolled her eyes in a show of anger and said something. I did not hear what she said because I was so thrilled by her sacred presence. I felt those sparkling eyes brimming with love and bliss.

When a mother cat holds her kitten by the scruff of its neck, the bite does not hurt. Similarly, even if Amma scolds us, her 'anger' will never harm us but only protect us from danger.

On another occasion, I quarreled with my teacher. Amma scolded me and told me to apologize. I did so. I count these occasions as blessings.

I was such a rogue! When I look back, I clearly see how Amma has shown me the right path and patiently corrected me all the way. I am still here only because of her patience. Amma says, "What enables the disciple to grow is the Guru's patience."

But these days, I find her rebukes harder to bear. It must be because my ego has taken over my child's heart. In the spiritual life, we must dig deep through layers of ego to recover the innocent child.

Isn't this what Amma is trying to make us do? Just as Śrī Rāmakṛṣṇa Paramahamsa shaped Narendra into Swāmī Vivēkānanda, Amma brought out the innocence and purity in her senior-most disciples. A child-like heart is evident in Swāmījī's words and actions. Amma often says that even if she scolds him severely, he continues to smile at her.

Amma has said that in the early days, she would fiercely drive away the first group of brahmacārīs and sit with her eyes shut, but they would innocently try to open her eyelids! Seeing this, her heart would melt and she would not be able to keep up her stern front any more.

A disciple strives to do the Guru's will and not make demands of the Guru. Amma has narrated how, when Swāmījī's pair of slippers broke, he did not get a new pair but went without slippers until Amma told him to buy a new pair. Such is the attitude of a disciple.

Once, Swāmījī presented a *hari-katha*[3] on the life of Śrī Rāmakṛṣṇa. While describing his pain of separation from Kālī, Swāmījī became so identified with the pangs of longing for the Divine Mother that he started calling out, "O Amma! Amma!

---

3 *Literally, the story (*katha*) of Hari (Lord Viṣṇu). A traditional form of discourse in which the narration is interspersed with singing.*

Where are you?" Amma could not resist the call. She came, caressed him and brought him back to an ordinary plane. Amma might well have been demonstrating through Swāmījī the attitude of a true devotee.

Amma has spoken about how she tied Swāmī Praṇavāmṛtānanda to a pillar, seeing him as child Kṛṣṇa. It was his innocence and love that made Amma see him as a child.

Once, Amma asked me why I loved the bhajan *'Nīlāmbuja nayanē.'* I said that it was because the song expresses intense love for Amma and that when I sing the bhajan, I, too, can feel the pain of separation Swāmījī felt. Such is the longing that even those who hear it will be touched by the same sentiment.

A few years ago, during a talk that Swāmījī gave during Amma's birthday celebrations, he said, "I was a flower adorning Amma's head. The flower had an intense desire to see Amma's holy feet. Thinking that it would be easy to do, it jumped down but could not find her feet! Even today, that flower is in search of Amma's feet!"

Swāmījī's visualization of himself as a flower on Amma's head touched me deeply. I understood it to mean that each one of us is somewhere on Amma's body. I began to wonder, "Where am I in Amma?" I became obsessed with this thought and would pray even as I went to sleep, "Amma, at least once, please show me where I am in you!"

On my birthday that year, one of my sisters gave me a photo of Amma; there was a child seated in her lap. Seeing this, I decided that I was in Amma's lap! From that day onwards, I began to meditate on the goal of being in her lap always. I even Photoshopped a childhood photo of myself seemingly seated in

Amma's lap and sent it to Amma when she was abroad. Amma kept it in her room for several years.

The following lines from Śrī Ōṭṭūr Uṇṇi Nanpūtirippāḍ's poem reinforced this longing:

> *āṭṭavum kazhiññ-amma tan maṭittaṭṭilēykk-ennu vīzhum ñān?*
> *vīṇum amma tan śītaḷāṅkattil sānandam enn-uṛaṅgum ñān?*
> O Amma, when the dance of life has ended, when will I fall into your lap? And when will I sleep blissfully in your cozy, maternal lap? (from *'Kaṇṇante Puṇya'*)

Amma affirmed this *saṅkalpa* (creative visualization) of mine. Once, when an āśram resident asked me to show Amma a picture of the Śiva *kuṭumbam* (Lord Śiva's family), I showed it to Amma and told her that I was Gaṇēśa, sitting on Pārvatī's lap! Another brahmacāriṇī, who was present, quipped that she was Muruga. Some days later, when Amma was returning to her room after bhajans, I showed her the picture again. Pointing to me, one of the brahmacāriṇīs said with some dismay, "Amma, she says that she is sitting in your lap; another sister says she is standing near you. Where are we?"

Amma smiled and said, "All of you, Amma's children, are in each and every one of Amma's hair follicles!"

These words were not only a confirmation of my saṅkalpa, I also understood that whatever we do affects Amma's body. Hasn't she said that her body suffers when our *sādhana* (spiritual practices) becomes lax? Why would Amma say this when she is not concerned about her own body? It is to drive home the point that Amma and her children are one. If we remain aware of this truth, we will never be able to make mistakes.

After meeting Amma, I began to go for all her bhāva darśans and found it increasingly difficult to stay away from her. The consecration of the Chennai Brahmasthānam Temple took place during my third-year degree examinations and I could not attend. Though I was feeling anguished about it, I told myself that Amma is always with me. While preparing for the exams, I listened to her bhajans. No one at home objected to this, as I had always done well academically. I had to sit for a total of eight papers for my degree in mathematics. I was determined to score full marks in all the papers and was sure that I would be able to do so; how conceited I was! Alas, in the first exam, I could answer only 30 of the 45 questions.

After submitting my answer sheet, I left the examination hall. Reaching home, I ran straight to the altar. Looking at Amma's photo, I asked her, "Amma, what happened to me? If this is what happens even after studying so hard, what's the use of continuing my studies?" I cried and cried, collapsed in front of Amma's photo, and fell asleep.

When I woke up, I was a different person. I felt refreshed and buoyed by an unknown self-confidence. I thought, "Wasn't I listening to Amma's bhajans while studying? She is always with me. So, why should I fear failure? I studied for the examinations and did what I could. Let Amma take care of the rest." With such an attitude, I continued preparing for the other exams.

The results were released a month later. I had scored full marks in the first examination, even though I had only answered 30 questions. To this day, this remains a mystery. The only explanation I have is Amma's divinity, which surpasses all understanding.

Amma has come to save us from the throes of worldly life. Let us not squander the good fortune we have had in meeting her and being guided by her to see the oneness of all in creation. Amma sings,

> *raṇḍalla ñānum ammayum ennamma ennōḍ-ōtiyirunn-ennālum*
> *onnāyi kāṇuvān kelppill-enikkennum paital āvān āṇu mōham*
> Though Amma has said that she and I are not separate, I lack the capacity to see that we are one. O Amma, I want only to be your child always. (from *'Hṛdaya-nivāsinī'*)

The reader would have noticed that I quoted lines from three bhajans in this talk. The day I finished preparing the talk, Amma sang *'Karuṇārdra-mānasam.'* I did not make much of it. The very next day, she sang *'Hṛdaya-nivāsinī.'* Two friends who had listened to me rehearsing my talk remarked upon the coincidence. I told them, "Yes, Amma sang two of the bhajans I mentioned. But there's one more. Will Amma sing that tomorrow?" The next day, she sang *'Kaṇṇante Puṇya.'* The synchronicity was uncanny!

Lord Kṛṣṇa told Arjuna, "I have already killed the enemies; you just need to be an instrument in my hands" (*Bhagavad Gītā*, 11.33). Similarly, Amma prepared all these satsaṅgs. All we need to do is to allow her words to be spoken through us. When we cultivate a child-like heart, the ego recedes, and we can allow the Lord to work through us. May the innocence and love of a child-like heart dawn in us all.

4

If We Take One Step

Swāmī Vijayāmṛtānanda Puri

Once upon a time, there was an old piano in a palace. The king, who inherited it from his late father, had grown up listening to the music of this piano. Its tone used to be beautiful and unique, but the piano was in a very bad shape. The king wanted to listen to the piano once again, and so, he invited expert piano technicians to repair the old piano. They worked day and night, but couldn't restore it.

One day, an old man came to the entrance of the palace. With his tattered clothes, long hair and beard, he looked like a beggar. He told the gatekeeper, "I heard there is an old piano here that is not producing music. I can fix it."

Hearing this, the gatekeeper smiled. So many experts had tried to repair the piano but all of them had failed. What miracle could this beggar possibly do? Nevertheless, the old man's words had a ring of authority to them. So, the gatekeeper took him to the king. He thought, "Let the king decide."

The old man said, "My Lord, I was told that the piano is already in a bad shape. So, it can't hurt if we try to fix it one more time."

Conceding to his logic, the king allowed the old man to work on the piano. He worked day and night for several days. One night, a beautiful melody was heard in the palace. The king was asleep but when he heard the music, he woke up at once. He recognized the tone of the old piano! He came rushing to the room where the piano was kept. He couldn't believe his eyes: the old man was playing the piano! Amazed, the king said, "You did a wonderful job! How did you fix it? It must have been very difficult."

The old man said, "It is true that it took some effort to fix it but it was not difficult for me because I made this piano long ago when your father was king. You were just a small boy."

The king asked him what he wanted in return for his wondrous gift. The old man said, "I don't need anything. My only wish is that my creation should produce music all the time."

The creator can easily fix his creation. Are we not all damaged instruments that have lost their tune? We are souls who lost our 'tuning' with the supreme consciousness at some point in time. Amma, the compassionate creator, has accepted not just one or two but tens of thousands of damaged instruments to her divine workshop. A few can be repaired quickly. They just need a little dusting and tweaking to reproduce music. The others might require much more time and effort, depending on the degree of damage. But for Amma, it is not a difficult task, because she is the creator. She knows the secret of creation and where her creation has gone wrong.

We are all fortunate to have been admitted to this divine workshop. We might have come under the hands of many 'experts.' But they could not fix our problems because the problems are not simple. Hence, we need the help of the creator herself.

One of the mantras in the *Lalitā Sahasranāma*, the 1,000 names of the Divine Mother, is, "*Ōm sṛṣṭikartryai namaḥ*" — "I bow down to the Divine Mother, who is the creator" (264). Amma knows the secret of creation. She has alluded to this many times. When someone asked her about how she knew so many details about worldly life, Amma answered, "The manufacturer knows more about the car than the driver."

Amma knows everything about us. Therefore, she can solve all our problems. But just like the king in the story, we must keep the door to our hearts wide open to receive Amma when she knocks. Our ego is like the king. We must have the humility to allow Amma to work on us. Only if we have this attitude of surrender can we gain true victory in life.

My life with Amma has taught me that the Guru's role cannot be explained in words. The word 'Guru' has been defined thus:

> *yo dharmyān śabdān gṛnātyupadiśati saḥ guru*
> The Guru is one who uplifts the disciple by dispelling ignorance, promoting righteousness and truthfulness, and granting Self-knowledge.

Isn't our beloved Amma doing the same thing? We must have seen how a mother teaches her toddler to walk. She stands in front of the child, holding its hands as she walks backwards. This is how the child moves forward. The mother is happy to move backwards for the sake of her child. Amma also does the same thing, with patience and sacrifice. She thus leads us to spiritual heights. Only a great master like Amma can lead us like this.

One can find numerous statements in the Vēdas that emphasize the necessity of a Guru for one who wishes to progress spiritually. These days, Amma spends at least four hours a day with us. Her presence is the greatest satsaṅg. Each and every phase of my life with her has been sacred, purely because of that association with her. Amma has showered her grace profusely on me. The various experiences that I have had by her grace remind me of Amma's saying, "Grace bestows what skill cannot."

I will share a few experiences pertaining to this topic. The following incident happened more than 20 years ago, during one of Amma's Brahmasthānam programs. Typically, an āśram resident gives a talk before Amma comes to the stage. That day, it was my turn to speak. Though I had no experience in public speaking, I did not prepare for the talk.

I went to the stage and began my first ever public talk. After 10 minutes, I noticed that the microphone had stopped working. I thought there was a power failure. After a while, I tapped the mic but it was still not working. That is when I noticed that the lights and fans were still on. That meant that there was no power failure.

Later, I learned that Amma had, out of compassion for the audience, ordered my mic to be turned off! I felt depressed, humiliated and shocked. In hindsight, I realized that it had been a shock treatment. It seems that all of us need such treatments at times. A shock treatment from Amma is never in vain.

This reminds me of a story from the life of Abraham Lincoln. Once, he wrote a letter to the school where his son was studying:

> Respected Teacher,
>
> Treat him gently; but do not cuddle him because only the test of fire makes fine steel...
>
> Teach him to learn to lose and also to enjoy winning...
>
> Teach him it is far more honorable to fail than to cheat...

Amma says that the disciple's defeat is actually a victory. I accepted defeat. But after that incident, my attitude changed. Until then, I had not thought it necessary to prepare for talks. I had foolishly presumed that ideas would flow once I was in front of the mic. After this incident, I started to take the task of public speaking seriously. I read, reflected and prepared.

After this, Amma asked me to speak on several occasions. There were times when I felt as if Amma spoke through me and thus made me her instrument.

I am reminded of an unforgettable incident. It took place in 2016, a few days before Amma's visit to Kolkata. I was visiting a prestigious center for research on Sanātana Dharma, Indology, Sanskrit Language and Eastern thought. Managed by the Ramakrishna Mission, this institution is popular in Kolkata. There is a spiritual discourse in one of the auditoriums daily, and the talk draws 400 – 500 people. The speakers are usually swāmīs and scholars from the Ramakrishna Mission; rarely is anyone outside that circle invited to speak. I had gone there to invite the swāmī in charge of that center, for Amma's darśan.

While talking to him, he suddenly asked me if I would give a talk. He said that I could choose the topic. He asked me to deliver the lecture on April 8th, and Amma was arriving in Kolkata on April 12th. Even though this did not give me much time to prepare, I felt that I should not miss this opportunity to introduce Amma to a new audience. So, I agreed.

The days ahead were hectic. I became caught up with matters pertaining to Amma's visit. I could not prepare for the speech until the day of the talk. That morning, I had to go to Durgapur for urgent meetings. The venue of the talk was nearly 200 kilometers away or about four hours' drive from Durgapur. The only time I had to prepare my talk was during the drive back.

We left Durgapur at 1:30 p.m. The talk was scheduled for 6 p.m. I took a notepad and a pen and closed my eyes to pray. That was the last thing I remember. Out of exhaustion, I fell into a deep sleep. The devotee accompanying me thought, "Let him rest." He compassionately instructed the driver not to honk and disturb my sleep.

I woke up only when my phone rang. It was a call from the Ramakrishna Center. When I saw that it was already 5:45 p.m., I panicked! The driver reassured me that we could reach the venue on time. But I thought, what is the point in being on time when I have nothing to deliver? I started crying. I felt as if I were about to sit for an examination completely unprepared. I began to perspire in the air-conditioned car. I prayed to Amma for help.

Then something unusual happened. All of a sudden, I became calm and composed. I felt a torrential flow of ideas in my mind and noted everything down. I recalled two or three short stories from my college days. In addition, two or three examples, two jokes, and three incidents came to mind. Altogether, I had 12 good points for an hour's talk. When I revised the speech, I found that it was in order and there was no need to edit it. It was as if someone had prepared a talk on my behalf and implanted it in my head. Usually, preparing a talk takes me up to a week. But this job was completed in just 15 minutes.

We reached the venue. I had to go the stage straight away. The auditorium was full. You could hear a pin drop. Praying to Amma, I started speaking.

When I finished, there was rapturous applause. Many people came to thank me for the talk. A few even gave me *dakṣiṇa* (honorarium). What made me even happier was seeing many of them at Amma's program four days later. Who else but Amma could have helped me in those crucial 15 minutes?

This was a memorable experience of how Amma makes us an instrument in her hands. That day, I understood the real meaning of the following verse from the *Bhagavad Gītā:*

> *tasmāt tvam uttiṣṭha yaśo labhasva jitvā śatrūn bhuṅkṣva rājyaṁ samṛddham*
> *mayaivaite nihatāḥ pūrvam eva nimitta-mātraṁ bhava savya-sācin*
>
> Therefore, arise and acquire glory. Conquer your enemies and enjoy a prosperous kingdom. They have already been killed by me. O Arjuna, just be an instrument. (11.33)

If we have an attitude of surrender, Amma will be on our side and take over. She resides within us and works through us. I use this opportunity to express my deepest gratitude to Amma for her grace. I also ask her to forgive me for not being prepared. I know that I ought to have been more prepared, but somehow, the situation was such that I found myself strapped for time.

When I compare and contrast these two incidents — my first talk in public and this one — I see that if Amma had not given me the shock treatment by having my mic turned off, I would not have reached this point. Since then, Amma has been trying to teach me the basic lessons of karma yōga. By guiding me to bring purity into my actions, she is making me worthy of her grace.

Whether big or small, Amma does everything for us. She does not expect anything in return except our spiritual growth. But are we taking steps to progress spiritually? Are we doing anything to reciprocate her boundless love? No. In truth, we are often miserly in our spiritual life.

There is a popular Bengali poem called *Kripon* by the great poet Rabindranath Tagore. In Bengali, *'kripon'* means 'miser.' The poem is based on a beautiful story. Once, there was a poor, old man who lived alone in a small hut. He was a devotee of the Lord. He lived on the alms he obtained by begging. One day while returning home after begging, he saw the king in a beautiful chariot. He thought, "If I get alms from the king, I will never have to beg again for the rest of my life." With that thought in mind, he approached the king. But the king did not give him anything. Instead, he alighted from the chariot and stretched out his hands to the beggar for alms. Disappointed and dejected, the beggar thought, "What should I do? The king is begging for alms from me! I don't have anything except a handful of rice. If I offer it, I'll have to hungry the whole day. But if I don't give the king anything, I could be punished. After all, he is the king!"

Hesitantly, he opened his small bundle of rice and offered the king a single grain of rice. He then left. When he returned to his hut, he opened the bundle. To his astonishment, he saw a grain of gold. He realized that the man he encountered was not the king, but the King of all kings, the Almighty in human guise! The beggar realized his mistake. He thought, "I gave him just one grain and he returned a grain of gold. Had I given him all that I had, I would have been blessed with so much wealth. I should not have been so miserly."

If we give God one thing, in His compassion, He will return it a thousand-fold. Similarly, Amma says that if we take one step towards her, she will take a hundred steps towards us.

But we are misers, like the beggar. We don't want to make any effort. We don't want to give her our hearts. In fact, we don't understand the rare blessings we enjoy.

About 10 years ago, I visited Uttarkashi for some āśram work. The work was supposed to take just one day, but owing to landslides and heavy rains, the roads connecting to the mainland had been washed away. I was trapped there for 10 days. I visited the old āśrams in the area to meet the monks there so that I could have the benefit of their holy company. When they learned that I was from Amma's āśram, they said, "You are lucky! You have a Guru in the female form, and that, too, as a Mother. We haven't been blessed with this rare opportunity."

It is said that when God assumes a human form, all the rivers flow towards her holy feet, all the mountains prostrate to her, and all the stars circumambulate her. Being able to live with a great master like Amma, who is revered by all of nature and by the whole universe, is a rare privilege. But we often don't appreciate the blessings we have received in having met Amma and come under her guidance.

It has been said, "Do not love the one who is beautiful to the world. Love the one who makes your world beautiful." Many of us fall in love with those who are physically beautiful. We ought to love the person who makes our inner, spiritual world beautiful. Amma beautifies both our inner and outer worlds. She is beautiful and can make our world beautiful too. Therefore, let us direct all our love towards Amma. May our hearts ever flow towards her holy feet.

5

In the Shelter of Her Arbor

Br. Cidghanāmṛta Caitanya

We have been blessed to meet Amma, the incarnation of love. We did not have to perform any ritual or undergo any difficult austerity in order to meet her. Many have taken refuge in the cool and shady arbor of pure love where the blissful flowers of Amma's tenderness blossom.

The Guru's advent is like the efflorescence of spring in a desert. Anyone can lay down the burdens of life at Amma's feet. They can tell her their countless sorrows and seek her guidance. Amma is like a giant mountain unshaken by any storm. She performed tremendous *tapas* (austerities) to relieve the sorrow of this world. Her darśan is a wonder. Amma's touch and hugs are *mahā-dīkṣās* (great spiritual initiations) that awaken goodness in a world ruled by selfishness, doubt, infidelity and rivalry. Amma is scripting an immortal saga of unconditional love and service that will inspire eloquence in poets, historians and orators in times to come.

Motherhood is a sacrifice beyond comprehension. A Guru is a truth beyond words. Amma is the Guru of gurus and the epitome of motherhood. She is a source of comfort, guidance and the abode of peace in the world today.

Amma wants to give us more than temporary relief. She wants to elevate us to the realization of the ultimate truth.

The ancient *ṛṣis* (seers) of India blessed the whole universe by showering the nectar of pure love. This universal love or attitude of oneness is the harmonic drone behind India's eternal melody. The ṛṣis found their true calling in revealing to humanity their innate divinity. They perceived this truth through logic and direct experience, and conveyed it through the *śrutis* (Vēdas). This wisdom has been passed through the ages and continues to attract seekers even today. This philosophy transcends the boundaries of time, religion, creed, caste, nationality and gender. Amma, the living embodiment of universal love, is attracting the attention of the whole world.

The Guru is like a fire of wisdom. We enter this fire when we become a disciple. When we constantly meditate on the purity of our Guru, wisdom will dawn in our hearts. Our *vāsanās* (latent tendencies) will get burned up and we will attain the timeless state of salvation.

A Guru reveals her grace through experiences imparted to the disciples. I have had many such experiences, but I will describe just a few of them.

One evening, I was walking through my village when I heard a bhajan from one of the houses: '*Cāmuṇḍāyē Kālī Mā...*" I stopped and then went straight to the house and asked who sang that bhajan. A man there told me that an 'Amma' from Kollam by the name of Mata Amritanandamayi sang it. I asked, "From where did you get this cassette?"

He said, "From a man named Mohanan, who works at the water supply department."

I went to meet him. He told me more about Amma. A week later, I heard that he had arranged a trip from Kannur to the Amṛtapuri Āśram for 50 people at ₹100 each. I gave him the money without a second thought and secured my seat.

At that time, I was an activist in the Communist Party. I had no faith in God. I still don't know why I wanted to meet Amma.

My maiden journey to the āśram was in the evening. Most of my fellow travelers were in their 60s. I was the only young man among them. They were doing *nāma-japa* (chanting of divine names) throughout the trip. I found it annoying because I couldn't sleep.

The bus reached Vallikavu at 6 a.m. Someone suggested that all of us line up and walk into the āśram while chanting. I began to simmer with irritation. Seeing us chanting, some of the locals started laughing. This was almost too much for the atheist and the communist in me.

At that time, there was little by way of accommodation in the āśram. We kept our luggage in the Kālī Temple and slept next to it. After a shower and breakfast, we stood in the darśan line. Mothers let their children lie in their laps only until a certain age. But Amma allows all her children, regardless of how old they are, to lie in her lap. I stared at that incredible scene, where old people became like little babies. When it was my turn to lie in her lap, Amma whispered "*ponnu mōnē*" ("precious son") three times into my ears. To tell the truth, I felt nothing in particular. After darśan, I went to the Kālī Temple. My mind became agitated and I felt an overwhelming fear. I shut my eyes tightly and lay there. I did not eat all afternoon or at night. I sat in a corner with my eyes closed during bhajans and slept right there when they ended.

The tour group decided to leave after Amma's darśan the next day. All those people who came along with me went for darśan on the second day too. I did not. I was feeling completely disconcerted. I did not eat or bathe. After I boarded the bus, I opened my eyes only after reaching Kannur. My fellow travelers invited me to visit different temples on the way, but I declined. When I reached home, I was bedridden for a week. I lost five kilograms. I took a vow never to visit Amma's āśram again.

A week passed. The desire to see Amma again grew in my mind until I could no longer bear it. I took a train to Vallikavu without deliberating on the decision. Like a wisp of cotton wool being carried away by a strong current, some uncontrollable desire and excitement drove me towards Amma. Soon, I started going to Vallikavu twice a week. Opposition began to brew at home and in my community. The local communist party, to which I was so devoted, expelled me. But by that time, I was sure about the purpose of my life, and my mind never wavered. Amma says that if our goal is clear, all the roadblocks will be cleared. My bad habits also started to drop away, one by one.

I would go to the āśram 10 days before Amma's birthday celebrations and engage in a variety of service activities. I used to immerse myself in the construction of public toilets for visiting devotees. It was a huge task. The toilets were constructed by placing sheets on top of pits that were dug deep. After the celebrations, I would go back home only after I had finished filling and covering those pits. At night, I would sleep comfortably on a mat outside the huts where the brahmacārīs used to live.

In 1993, on a bright *Ōṇam*[4] morning, I set out for Vallikavu. I reached Oachira and was about to board a bus when a van stopped near the bus. The driver of that van was a friend. He told me that he was going to Vallikavu. I gladly got in. When we arrived, Amma was about to leave for Chicago to attend the Parliament of World Religions. Devotees stood in line to see her off. I eagerly joined the line. Amma touched my hands on her way out.

After Amma left, the āśram felt empty; so did my mind. I had planned to stay for two days but visitors were not allowed to stay in the āśram when Amma was not there. I had to leave. My friend was kind enough to give me a lift in his van. Seeing my sorrow, he said, "Let's go via Nedumbassery. Some devotees go to the airport to see Amma off, and she usually gives them darśan."

We sped to the airport. Amma was giving darśan to people in her car. When I went for darśan, she asked me, "Son, why are you so distressed?"

I couldn't answer. A tide of difficult feelings was flowing through my mind. I went to the balcony to watch Amma's plane leave.

Suddenly, many of the airport staff started rushing towards a plane that had just landed. I was told that the plane had struck an eagle. It was the plane that Amma was on. The flight was postponed to 4 a.m. the next morning. Someone informed us that she was calling āśram residents to her room. Though I wasn't a resident, I tagged along. I sat down next to Amma and told her that I had arrived late at the āśram because my mother had asked me to stay for the traditional Ōṇam feast. Amma

---

4 *Kerala's biggest festival, occurring in the month of Chiṅṅam* (August *– September).*

said that my ardent prayers had caused the eagle incident and delayed her flight! This incident convinced me that God does not hesitate to become a servant of a devotee.

In 1996, I asked Amma if I could stay on as a brahmacārī. She said, "You're just interested in sitting with your eyes closed, but karma yōga is more important here. You must serve sincerely. Think deeply and give me an answer by tomorrow: to stay or not."

I spent the whole day thinking about it but couldn't arrive at a decision. The next day, I went in a confused state to see Amma. She asked me "Son, what did you decide?"

"I've decided to do what Amma wants me to do."

Thus, I gave her the responsibility of making the decision. She said, "Go and tell Ānandāmṛta (now Swāmī Amṛtātmānanda Puri) that Amma has allowed you to stay in the āśram as a brahmacārī. Ask him to make you serve in the press," she added.

I had never even seen a printing press until then. About 20 brahmacārīs were serving in the press at the time. Amma talks about smoothening the rough edges of rocks and polishing them by putting them all in one tumbler. Our motley crew of different cultures, characters, and traits had its sharp edges smoothed out through this sēvā.

Āśram residents used to fast on Saturdays. In the evening, there would be a *satsaṅg* (spiritual discourse) by a brahmacārī or brahmacāriṇī under the 'Green Roof' of the Kālī Temple. After the satsaṅg, Amma would serve everyone *pāyasam* (pudding). I went along with everyone but was stopped by a brahmacārī, who said "This meeting is for āśram residents only. Please leave." I explained that Amma had allowed me to stay as a brahmacārī, but he did not let me in. After the satsaṅg, Amma came downstairs and sat in a chair. I managed to sit close to her feet. She asked for the pāyasam to be brought down. Amma thus transformed my anguish at being denied permission to attend the satsaṅg into a sweet experience. Her mind can hear even the feeblest calls of distress.

After I became a brahmacārī, I went on my first North Indian tour. We left at 6 a.m. and stopped for tea at the Thamarasseri Churam (mountain pass) 12 hours later. In those days, Amma used to make the tea and serve it herself. These chai stops were an opportunity for us to ask questions and clear our doubts. Although I had a question, I remained silent out of fear.

After the chai stop, the group set off again. After a while, the bus suddenly stopped. Amma had stopped her car. She got out, boarded our bus, and came straight to where I was sitting with another brahmacārī. We both stood up to give our seats to her, but Amma told me sweetly, *"Mutte, aviḍe irikkū!"* ("Darling child, sit there!"). Saying so, she sat down beside me.

I took this as an opportunity to ask her, "Amma, which is greater: the Guru's grace or our own effort?"

Amma replied, "Grace is greater than effort. But effort is also needed. Only lazy people say that effort is not needed."

This experience showed me that the Guru knows a disciple inside out. The question that arose in my mind drew Amma towards me. Lord Kṛṣṇa says:

> *idam śarīram kauntēya kṣētram ityabhidhīyatē*
> *ētad yō vētti tam prāhuḥ kṣētrajña iti tadvidaḥ*
> O Arjuna, this body is called the *kṣētra* (the field of activities). The knower of this body is called *kṣētrajña* by sages, who have discerned the truth about both.
> (*Bhagavad Gītā*, 13.2)

The body is presented as the *kṣētra* (field), and the *ātma*, as the spirit that lends vigor to this field. The ego-consciousness or the 'I' is this *kṣētrajña*. This 'I' dwells in all beings.

A field is where seeds are sown and harvested. After the seed sprouts, branches, leaves and flowers develop. When the eternal *jīva* (soul) falls into this field, it sprouts an individuality, with its own worldly interests and *vāsanās* (latent tendencies). We reap what we sow, both sorrow and joy. We cannot plant the seed of evil and expect a harvest of goodness. A seed that is fried will not sprout. A seeker ought to burn the seeds of vāsanās in the fire of tapas.

Our life is a chariot harnessed to the horses of thoughts, words and deeds. If these horses run in different directions, we will be done for! Our goal is salvation. So, we must direct the chariot of life towards this goal. It is foolish to imagine that we can reach our goal by changing our direction. The impediments on this path are created by none other than our own mind. When we direct these horses along a single path, we can reach the goal of life.

To do so, we must use our powers of *icchā, jñāna* and *kriya*—resolve, knowledge and action. But before that, we need to exhaust our cravings for worldly pleasures. Often, our mind becomes submerged by the tidal waves of emotions generated by desires. Like a ship without a rudder, we are unable to cross the ocean of *samsāra* (worldliness). We may have the desire to escape, but we need to put in effort and undergo some *tyāga* (sacrifice) to achieve it. Scholarship will not help us cross the ocean of samsāra. Wisdom is what is needed. Merely quoting the scriptures without assimilating its wisdom makes us no better than a parrot. But if we apply ourselves sincerely, wisely and prudently, we will make spiritual progress.

The word *kṣētra* also implies *kṣīyate*—that which perishes. The body is *śīryate*—one that is shed or which falls away. Both the temple and body are perishable. Our biggest mistake is thinking that we are this perishable body. This is ignorance. We must understand the impermanence of our body through *swādhyāya* (self-inquiry) and tapas. The ego—which can arise through body consciousness, high self-esteem or even pride in our ancestry—is not the imperishable *ātmā* (Self).

Identifying with the body and mind is folly. Once we overcome this false identification and contemplate on the true nature of things, we will begin to see the light of consciousness. We will realize that we are the eternal *kṣētrajña* and not the ephemeral *kṣētra*. We gain the unshakeable conviction that we are the Supreme: *'ayam ātmā brahma.'*

Vāsanās prevent us from seeing the underlying unity of the all-pervading consciousness. Pure consciousness is a witness to everything. But the fog of pride and ego obscures it. Trapped inside our rooms, we perceive the vast sky as divided by the walls of our individuality. In the bhajan *'Ōmkāra Divya Poruḷē,'* Amma sings:

> *ennile ñān āṇu nīyum*
> *pinne ninnile nī āṇu ñānum*
> *kaṇṇu kāṇāykayāl bhinnamāy tōnnunnu*
> *bhinnam allennāl itonnum*
> You are the 'I' in me, and I am the 'you' in you.
> But unable to see this, we perceive diversity, though there is only unity.

Amma says that spirituality begins and ends with compassion. When compassion becomes the core of life, the barrier between 'I' and 'you' collapses. One who sees that his own Self is in all beings is able to see all beings as his own. This is the essence of Amma's teachings. We should serve creation with dignity and modesty, seeing it as God's body. Our mortal bodies may burn out like a charred wick, but we can glow and give light and fragrance to the world like a lighted lamp or incense stick.

Amma's mission is to provide support and shade to all living beings in this world. She is one with the cosmos. The river of love within her flows unobstructed. Her life is an open textbook for us to study and understand the purpose and magnitude of human life. When the feeling of oneness becomes deep-rooted, compassion becomes the driving force behind life. When we look at the world with eyes of mercy, we will get a better view. This beautiful universe will become our temple. When separate notions of 'I' and 'you' vanish, we will see the Self in everything.

Amma says that spirituality is nothing but the principle of surrender. Lord Kṛṣṇa says the same thing in the *Gītā*:

> *sarva-dharmān parityajya mām ēkam śaraṇam vraja*
> *aham tvām sarva-pāpēbhyō mōkṣayiṣyāmi mā śucaḥ*
> Abandon all other *dharmas* (duties) and surrender to me alone.
> I shall save you from all sins. Do not fear. (18.66)

Amma often says, "Whatever you do, you should have the attitude that God alone is making you act." That is what '*mām ēkam śaraṇam vraja*' means. Dharma is what upholds this universe. Creation emanates from the one Self, also known as Brahman. Dharma determines the features, character and nature of everything in creation. Lord Kṛṣṇa tells Arjuna: *manmanā bhava*' ('Think of Me constantly') (18.66). How to do that? By remembering that God rules, guides and controls everything, and that we cannot be separated from Him even for a moment. Self-realization happens when we move from plurality to oneness. Then we see only Brahman in everything. A Self-realized man can never say, "I am doing this." He will see himself only as an instrument in God's hands. This surrender happens when all traces of our ego disappear. The goal of all spiritual striving is surrender. May we all be blessed to have this attitude of surrender.

6

The Attractiveness of Śraddhā

Bri. Varapradāmṛta Caitanyā

All of us are familiar with *pūjās* (forms of ritualistic worship) and *hōmas* (fire rituals). We offer ghee, grains, milk and other items to the sacrificial fire. Once burnt, we can no longer identify the quantity or quality of any of the materials offered. In the same way, good and bad *karmas* (actions) are reduced to ash in the fire of knowledge. This includes all types of karmas:

- *sañcita*: the sum of our past-life karmas, which form our tendencies.
- *prārabdha:* the karmas that are responsible for the experiences in our present birth.
- *āgāmi:* the karmas that we are now doing and the fruits of which we will taste in a future birth.

This fire of knowledge is the only thing that can liquidate our karmas. As spiritual seekers, we must learn how to kindle that fire. This is addressed in the *Bhagavad Gītā:*

> *śraddhāvān labhatē jñānaṁ tatparaḥ samyatēndriyaḥ*
> *jñānaṁ labdhvā parāṁ śāntim acirēṇādhigacchati*
> One who has full faith, devotion and control over his senses attains knowledge. Having attained it, he soon attains everlasting peace. (4.39)

We can attain this knowledge by having *śraddhā*, which refers to the mind's disposition to receive this knowledge. A person with śraddhā is always preparing to receive this knowledge. Once the knowledge is received, Self-realization takes place spontaneously. Once attained, it can never be concealed. That knowledge will shine brightly, like a lamp. The scriptures say that a person cannot pursue this knowledge; rather, it is knowledge that chooses the person with supreme faith.

The mind of a person with śraddhā always dwells on spiritual matters. The scriptures compare the mind to a river because it flows incessantly. Sometimes, it flows towards faith, and at other times, it flows in the opposite direction. In his commentary on the *Yōga Sūtras*, Sage Vyāsa says that the mind that flows towards faith leads that individual to spiritual liberation. In the Upaniṣads, this flow is called *jāgrat* (wakefulness.) Once we become wakeful, no further effort is needed to make spiritual progress. For someone who is alert, the whole world will be a Guru.

Amma often says that her Guru was Damayanti-amma, her mother, who was the very epitome of attentiveness. Although Amma never needed a Guru, she accepted every experience as her Guru. Amma's faith was based on the unshakeable conviction that she and this universe are not separate.

Śraddhā implies a willingness to learn from anyone or anything. Nature provides answers to all our problems. Amma recounts an experience from her early days that exemplifies this. It took place when Amma had just started giving Kṛṣṇa and Dēvī Bhāva darśans. Amma's family, which was orthodox, found it hard to accept her *bhāvas* (divine moods). Her father, Suguṇacchan, was feeling ashamed of how some people were criticizing Amma. One day, Amma heard that he was planning to leave home. Feeling sad, she thought, "He need not go anywhere. I shall leave instead. I don't want to create any problems for them." At that very moment, a piece of paper flew from somewhere and landed at her feet. It was a scrap from an old newspaper. Amma picked it up and read about how a young woman who had left home had been sexually harassed. Amma took it as a warning and dropped the idea of leaving. Amma has complete clarity about what to do and does not need to read a newspaper article for answers. She tells this story only to show us how someone who has faith can get all their answers from life.

Karma done in slipshod fashion creates sorrow for us and others. There is no point in blaming God when we have to face sorrow because of our own carelessness. Amma illustrates the importance of alertness through the following anecdote.

Patients in a particular bed in the intensive care unit of a hospital used to die every Sunday at 11 a.m. This was a mystery for the doctors. Some of them even believed that a supernatural power was at work. They appointed a team of experts to study the problem. The next Sunday, this team of doctors and nurses waited anxiously outside the ward. At exactly 11 a.m., a cleaner who worked only on Sundays entered the ward. He went straight to that bed, unplugged the life support machine, and plugged in the vacuum cleaner. Thus, the supernatural mystery was solved with a most mundane explanation.

The importance of śraddhā is mentioned again in the *Bhagavad Gītā*:

> *aśraddhayā hutaṁ dattaṁ tapas-taptaṁ kṛtaṁ ca yat*
> *asad ity-ucyatē pārtha na ca tat prētya nō iha*

> O son of Pṛthā, any sacrifice or penance done without faith is considered *'asat.'* They are useless both here and hereafter. (17.28)

Amma used to say, "Children, whenever Amma sees someone working with attentiveness, she feels like abducting that person! One who has śraddhā gains everything. Such is the greatness of this quality."

During a tour in North India, we were having lunch in a field with Amma. Amma brought up an incident from the previous day. While giving a talk in the Delhi Āśram, someone had entered the hall. Amma noticed him immediately and mentioned that she couldn't take her eyes off him. She then asked us why she had felt such a strong attraction towards him. No one could provide a satisfactory answer. Amma explained, "That person does all of his actions with utmost awareness. That's what drew me to him."

There is a strong magnetic power in śraddhā. It can cause water to flow into a desert or enliven a stone idol. Let me tell you how Amma breathed life into the stone idol that I was.

The first sēvā I was assigned in the āśram was to look after the cows. Someone would come to milk the cows at 4 am. I had to clean the cowshed, bathe the cows, give them water and hay, and have the cows ready before he arrived. I did all this systematically but in a mechanical manner. I still remember that I never used to show any love or affection to those poor animals.

I also had sēvā in the printing press. Once, when there was a lot of work to be done in the press, Amma came there one evening after bhajans to help us. I was sitting in front of Amma while folding the paper mechanically, looking at her without blinking, and chanting my mantra. But I had no śraddhā in my sēvā. Even while looking at Amma, I was not aware that she was watching me. After some time, Amma called out, "Hey, look! See how someone is folding the paper!" She then started imitating me. Amma took the paper very slowly, brought the edges together, folded it in the middle, turned the paper, and folded it once again. She took almost two minutes to fold just one sheet of paper! I became aware of how I was working. Amma was holding a mirror in front of me so that I could see myself. She taught me like this on many occasions.

Amma also guided me to turn inwards. One Tuesday morning, I did all my sādhana: *arcana* (chanting of the divine names), *japa* (repeated chanting of mantra) and meditation. I also observed silence. But that night, I felt sad thinking that Amma had not looked at me even once. I went to sleep thinking that there was no use doing sādhana.

That night, Amma came into my dream and said, "Oh, you did so many arcanas today! But did you remember me even once while chanting any of the mantras? Did you offer any mantras to my feet?" I woke up remembering the dream and realized that Amma was right. I was doing my sādhana mechanically and without any awareness. In this way, Amma pointed out my lack of awareness and helped me rectify the problem.

When a poet writes with great feeling, choosing his words with care, we enjoy the poem because of his śraddhā. We appreciate the beauty of a painting when the artist has painted it with śraddhā. Śraddhā elevates every action and makes it spiritual. Imagine how much śraddhā is needed to realize the subtle truths in the Guru's words and the scriptures!

Amma often gives the example of Bhīma from the *Mahābhārata*, and says that we need that kind of śraddhā. Even as children, the Kauravas were trying to get rid of the Pāṇḍavas, especially Bhīma, who was the mightiest. They tried to kill him several times by poisoning him and resorting to other means. Bhīma foiled all their attempts. But this naturally made him very alert. He never trusted the treacherous Kauravas and took extreme care with each step. Whenever he walked anywhere, he would examine the ground carefully for traps. His śraddhā alerted the Pāṇḍavas to the fact that the palace they had entered was made of lac, which was combustible, and this helped them plan their escape from the fire.

Amma explains this in a simple manner. If a thorn pricks our feet, we will walk carefully. That alertness will save us later from a greater danger. This is true both externally and internally. Small emotional pains will make us more alert and save us from spiritual downfall.

My family and I met Amma for the first time in 1985 at Kodungalloor Temple. We could not go for darśan that day. The next year, when Amma came to visit a family in Kodungalloor, we went to their house. When Amma came out of the house and saw us waiting there, she stopped in front of us and lovingly asked, "Children, aren't you coming to the āśram?" Amma took a few steps, turned to us again, and said, "Come in Amma's vehicle!"

Amma was going for a program in the Kodungalloor Āśram. That day, we went to the āśram with Amma! On our way back, my father bought a biography of Amma. When I read about Amma's love for her children, I began to long for that divine love.

I wanted to join the āśram. How can we resist Amma when we experience her supreme love flowing towards us?

Our father never allowed us to go out alone. We were not even allowed to go to the Kodungalloor Temple, which was only 10 minutes away. When I found out that Amma's āśram was far away in Kollam, I began to worry. Kollam was like a foreign destination for us! My father used to go to Amṛtapuri several times a week to see Amma, but he never took any of us with him. I never imagined that I would be able to go to Amṛtapuri to see Amma.

In those days, I used to see Amma in my dreams and speak to her, especially on the days when my father went to Amṛtapuri. This may be because of my intense desire to see her. Amma would ask, "Daughter, why aren't you coming to the āśram? Amma hasn't seen you for a long time!"

Seeing Amma in my dreams comforted me. Whenever I had any doubts, Amma would give me answers in my dreams. In one dream, I asked her, "Amma, will you allow me to join the āśram?"

"I will let you join the āśram after three years," was her reply.

There is a Kṛṣṇa temple near our house that I used to visit daily. One night, I dreamt that I was in that temple. When I looked into the sanctum sanctorum, instead of the idol of Lord Kṛṣṇa, I saw Lord Kṛṣṇa himself standing there giving darśan just like Amma. That beautiful form of Kṛṣṇa is still in my heart. The Lord was giving darśan and prasād to each devotee there. When he saw me, he called out my name and caught hold of my hand. He gave me a beautiful picture of Amma and said, "This is verily me!" When Kṛṣṇa caught my hand, his nail cut my finger slightly. I hardly noticed it at that time, as I was so happy to get a picture of Amma. When I woke up, I did not remember the dream, but when I washed my face, I felt the sting in my finger and recalled the dream.

Amma started visiting our home whenever she came to Kodungalloor. Once, many people came unexpectedly to see Amma. We had cooked only enough food for Amma and her disciples. When my mother saw so many people, she feared that there would not be enough food for everybody. In the meantime, my father began to serve food to the guests. My mother started praying to Amma. At that moment, Amma came to the kitchen, took some rice and curry on a plate, and told her, "Now you can serve. There is enough food." We were surprised to see that there was still some rice left in that small pot even after everyone had been served.

It was on that day that Amma told my father, "Son, if you don't stop drinking, I will take all your daughters with me to the āśram." Amma kept her word and graciously accepted all three of us into the āśram.

I must confess that the way I joined the āśram was a bit reckless. In 1990, Amma had a program at Mattancherry, Ernakulam. When I went for the program, Swāminī Gurupriyāmṛta asked me, "Don't you want to join the āśram? Amma allowed all the Calicut children to join the āśram. Why don't you ask Amma?"

I was so disappointed to hear that because I'd already had darśan. There was no other opportunity to ask Amma that day. So, we devised a plan. Swāminī went to my father and said, "Amma asked Divya to come to the āśram. We are taking her with us." Thus, I went to the āśram without even a single spare set of clothes.

When I asked Amma if I could join the āśram, she refused, saying that she could not allow any more girls to stay there. But

I refused to go back. Whenever Amma saw me, she would say, "Did you not lie to your father to come here? Spiritual life is not as easy as you think."

I would whisper, "No, Amma, I won't go back! I won't go back!"

After three days, my father came to the āśram with a suitcase full of clothes for me. I had been hiding from Amma, fearing that she would send me home. But when my father came, Amma allowed me to stay. Amma granted my wish and allowed me to join the āśram, just as she had promised me in my dream, three years before.

Amma says, "Children, you should have the śraddhā of a soldier on the battlefield or a student in the examination hall. If you are alert in every action, that spiritual practice will surely take you to God."

Let us strive to practice śraddhā in all our actions. If we do so, Amma will abduct us as well! O Amma, please come into our hearts as śraddhā.

7

Surrender Unto Me Alone

Br. Ādidēvāmṛta Caitanya

Human life is full of conflicts. The outer Kurukṣētra War may have ended, not the inner one, because both the Kauravas and Pāṇḍavas — the good and the evil — are still within us. Luckily, Lord Kṛṣṇa is also here with us as Amma, the very personification of love.

Amma says, "Children, the āśram is a Kurukṣētra (battlefield). If you win here, you will never be defeated anywhere else in the world. What you get here, you will not get anywhere else."

True enough, my personal battles began as soon as I joined the āśram. The first thing Amma asked me after I joined the āśram was, "Have you decided to enter the battlefield?" It was only through her boundless kindness that I could overcome many obstacles and difficulties.

My first *sēvā* (selfless service) was in the cowshed. This sēvā was the right medicine for me, for I had a serious illness: many things disgusted me. If I saw or heard something disgusting, I wouldn't even be able to eat. During the rainy season, I wouldn't leave my house.

The initial days in the cowshed went smoothly, but thoughts that I had adapted were soon shattered. All the cows came down with diarrhea. The cowshed smelled terrible! The floor became slick and unsafe to walk on.

I wondered if I had given them too much cattle feed or if they had consumed a purgative. As I stood there in shock, my state was like that of Arjuna at the start of the Kurukṣētra War. Just as Arjuna's bow slipped from his hands, my cleaning tools fell from mine.

But I did not want to give up. I knew I had to find a way to overcome this challenge.

Suddenly, I felt a spurt of energy. I sprang into action, like Arjuna picking up his bow and shooting arrows. I began to clear the manure with my bare hands. After this experience, cleaning the cowshed became a joyful experience.

Just as a mother hen knows of the different stages of growth inside each of the eggs she is brooding on, the Guru knows how spiritually evolved we are. Just as the egg hatches eventually, when the soul ceases to identify with the body-mind-intellect complex, it breaks out of the shell of its ego and attains Self-realization.

To attain this supreme goal, we must first purify the mind. Sēvā helps us overcome our weaknesses, reduces our karmic burden, and exhausts our *vāsanās* (latent tendencies).

One of my weaknesses was fear. When I was young, I was afraid of many things—the dark, lightning, snakes... My mother told me to chant the 10 names of Arjuna whenever I felt fear inside: "Arjuna, Phālguṇa, Jiṣṇu, Kirīṭī, Śwētavāhana, Bībhatsu, Vijaya, Pārtha, Savyasāci and Dhanañjaya."

Even the mighty Arjuna had fears and weaknesses. Lord Kṛṣṇa needled Arjuna by using the word *klaibyam*, which is used to describe an impotent man, to stir him from his depressive state:

> *klaibyam mā sma gamaḥ pārtha naitat tvayyupapadyatē*
> *kṣudram hṛdaya-daurbalyam tyaktvōttiṣṭha parantapa*
> O Pārtha, caving in to this unmanliness is unbecoming of you. O conqueror of enemies, abandon this petty weakness and rise up! (2.3)

In the previous verse, Lord Kṛṣṇa says:

> *kutastvā kaśmalam idam viṣamē samupasthitam*
> *anārya-juṣṭam aswargyam akīrtikaram arjuna*
> O Arjuna, how has this delusion overpowered you in this critical moment? It's disgraceful and will not take you to heaven. (2.2)

Towards the end of his life, Napoleon Bonaparte said, "There are two powers in the world: the sword and the mind. In the long run, the sword is always beaten by the mind." One who falls prey to the mind's weaknesses is easily defeated by the world. But one who has mastered his mind becomes a master of the whole world.

A common characteristic of the mind is it often dwells in the past or the future. It is rarely present, as the following anecdote illustrates.

One day, a man and his wife were having dinner when the power went off. The wife lit a candle and they continued eating. Noticing that his wife was perspiring a lot, the husband asked, "Shall I switch on the fan?"

His wife said, "What's wrong with you? If you switch on the fan, the candle will go out!"

Both had completely forgotten that there was no electrical power! This is how we are, even in our waking state. A person who is awakened is always in the present moment.

There was a time in my life when I felt overwhelmed by the feeling that life was not worth living. It was then that Devadas (now Br. Nirvāṇāmṛta Caitanya) came into my life. A physical educator at the Kannur Central Jail School, he came to meet the physical educator at the school where I was working. When I saw him, I heard him say of me, “This man is meant to be in the āśram. He'll join the āśram soon!”

As I did not understand what he meant, I merely smiled at him before returning to my classroom.

After a while, I was transferred to another school. He came there looking for me and gave me a copy of Amma's biography. He also came several times later to give me Amma's audio cassettes. I thought he was crazy, and did not look at the book or listen to the cassettes.

Finally, tired of trying to convince me to meet Amma, he said, “I live in Kannur town. You're welcome to visit me anytime.”

I thought it was a good idea, as I had been thinking of moving from my hometown. When I went to meet him that evening, he told me, “You can stay here, if you wish.”

The next day, I packed my things and moved in with him. One day, he took me to a devotee's home to listen to devotional songs sung by Amma. Hearing her beautiful voice, I was touched. I had never heard such a voice in my life. On the way back, I asked if I would be able to meet Amma at her āśram.

He said, “Hard to say. Amma often travels outside the āśram for programs.”

I did not want to go all the way to Kollam unless I could meet Amma. I began to pray constantly to her: "You can go wherever you like, but please be at the āśram when I come to see you."

On the night of Saturday, October 31st, 1986, I boarded the train from Kannur. It was *Diwālī*, the festival of lights. That was the day the true light came into my life. As I was about to enter the āśram, Amma approached me. She said, "Son, Mother was waiting for you." After a pause, she repeated, "Mother was waiting for you after canceling a program in Ernakulam."

I was surprised! Did Amma really hear my prayers? Everybody prostrated to her. I had never prostrated to anyone in my life. But I prostrated at her feet, looking around to see if anyone was watching. During my first darśan at the hut, I did not feel like saying anything to Amma. She asked me if I was leaving after the Dēvī bhāva darśan. I said yes.

That evening darśan was inexplicably blissful. After I prostrated to her, Amma put my head on her lap for a long time. Then, she poured sacred water into my mouth and anointed the spot between my eyebrows with sandalwood paste. I mentally surrendered to Amma. At that time, I used to suffer from constant headaches and back pain as a result of an accident. I found it hard to sit down. Amma asked me if I had consulted any doctor. I told her that I had tried both allopathic medicine and Ayurveda. She gently rubbed my forehead and back, saying, "Let me check." Amma then said, "Son, don't worry. Amma will solve all your problems." She placed her palm on my head and said, "Amma will be with you forever." Ever since then, I feel that Amma is with me all the time.

After darśan, Amma asked me to sit near her. After some time, she called me over, handed me some sacred ash, and said, "Apply this. Everything will be all right."

I did not apply it; I swallowed it instead! The pain has not troubled me to this date. I had come with many problems, but after meeting Amma, I forgot everything and felt as if I were floating on air. The difficulties of the past became distant memories.

When I returned home, I started living as if I were in the āśram. I did *arcana* and *japa* without fail. I felt Amma's presence everywhere and smelled her sweet fragrance all the time. I became a frequent visitor to Amṛtapuri.

Although I never thought of staying in the āśram, Amma began to ask, "Why don't you stay here?"

I did not say anything but started contemplating that possibility. During one darśan, I said, "Amma, I'm fed up with life! I've no idea what to do." I was hoping that Amma might allow me to stay in the āśram.

Amma said, "Should I transfer you to a private school?"

I wondered how Amma knew that I was working for a government school. When I soon got transferred to a private school near my hometown, I thought at first that it was just a coincidence. But later, I realized that Amma was letting me know that she was taking care of all my needs.

Still, I did not join the āśram. Amma began to test me. I received a letter from Br. Nirvāṇāmṛtajī: "Amma has asked Asokan (my previous name) to get married if he wants to."

I became annoyed. I thought, "Why is she saying something like that?"

On my way to the āśram the following week, I kept praying to Amma, “Oh Amma, please don’t push me into marriage!”

During darśan, Amma laughed and said, “Amma has not come to trap anyone but to liberate everyone from all traps.”

Amṛtapuri was getting more and more crowded. I thought, “Soon, there won’t be any room for me. Amma has so many children. She won’t want me here anymore.”

When I went for darśan, Amma asked me, “Why don’t you stay here? At least take a few days of leave and stay here.”

This time, I did not think twice. I started staying in the āśram at once. The doctor cannot perform the surgery without admitting the patient.

After some time in the cowshed, I was transferred to the cloakroom. It was near the sinks, which Amma used to pass. I started cleaning that place as well and soon developed pride in my cleaning abilities. One day, I was standing in front of the cloakroom when Amma came. She went straight to the sink and stood there. I thought the place looked clean. Amma asked, “Who cleans this place?”

I stood still. Amma put her hand inside the drainpipe and pulled out a big handful of decomposing waste. My jaw dropped. I did not imagine that Amma would do such a thing in her white sari.

Usually, doctors administer anesthesia before performing the surgery. But Amma’s surgery is without anesthesia. However, the ‘pain’ she inflicts is a sweet blessing. I am reminded of two lines from *‘Manassē Nin Swantamāyi,’* which Amma often sings:

dayāmayiyākuṃ dēvī bhayarūpam eḍuttālum
padatāril kiḍakkuvor dhanyarāṇavar

Even when the Divine Mother assumes a ferocious form,

those who cling to Her feet are blessed indeed.

Amma cannot remain in that ferocious state for too long. She will revert to her affectionate motherly nature again. I am reminded of an incident from the *Rāmāyaṇa*.

One day in the forest, Lord Rāma was standing and talking to his brother Lakṣmaṇa, who noticed that Rāma's heavy bow was squishing a frog, which was struggling in pain. When Lakṣmaṇa pointed this out, Rāma picked up the frog at once and compassionately asked, "Why didn't you speak up when you were in pain?"

The frog was a spiritually illumined soul. He said, "When others hurt me, I call out your name: *Rāma! Rāma!* But when you're the one giving me the pain, who can I call? So, I accept this pain as a blessing."

The surgeries that Amma performs removes our inner negativities. Although they may be painful, Amma herself will give us the painkiller.

One day, I was fanning Amma during Dēvī Bhāva. Suddenly, she turned her head to one side, and the hand fan hit her crown. Amma looked at me intently. She took the hand fan from me and showed me how to fan, holding it closer to Her ears. That meant I would surely hit her crown again. But I did not want to disobey. I fanned the way she showed me. Again, Amma turned her head, and the fan hit her crown. Now she looked angry. She said, "It's true that I am your mother. But don't you dare touch Amma's crown!"

I felt numb. I handed the fan to someone else and started to massage her feet slowly. But Amma pulled her legs away. Once again, she said, "Don't you dare touch Amma's crown!"

I left the place, embarrassed. I was acutely conscious that people who knew me were watching. I thought to myself, "My āśram life is over. I must leave."

I left the next morning. But soon after I left, I realized that Amma's presence and love were always with me and that she had only been testing me. I came back to the āśram. The day's darśan was almost over. The hut was full of devotees. When I reached Amma, she told everyone, "This son hit Amma's crown yesterday."

I thought, "Amma still hasn't forgotten." Feeling upset, I put my head in her lap. In a gentle tone, Amma said, "Son, did you get scared? Amma was only testing you. I thought you had courage."

Although I was relieved to hear this, after that incident, I stopped doing that sēvā. Later, Amma asked me, "Why aren't you sitting near me these days?"

The answer that came to mind was, "A cat that has fallen into hot water once will not risk it again!" Instead, I said, "I don't wish to bother others."

When Amma asked me to do sēvā at the Inquiry Counter, I asked, "Amma, can I sit in a corner and do my *mantra japa*?"

Amma paused for a moment and said: "Let me speak to Gurudas (now Swāmī Gurupādāśritānanda)."

Fearing that I may get a much more difficult sēvā, I quickly replied. "Amma, I shall willingly do sēvā at the Inquiry Counter!"

Right now, I am doing compost sēvā. By Amma's grace, I now enjoy any sēvā assigned to me. If our mind is pure and the desire for liberation is intense, we will have no difficulty in invoking Amma's presence.

If we wish to escape the clutches of *samsāra* (cycle of births and deaths), we must do as the Guru says. When we surrender completely, we will spontaneously merge with the Supreme.

The scent of flowers spreads in the direction of the wind. But the perfume of Amma's grace permeates the world. May we all feel Amma's grace. May she lead us all to the Truth and awaken us from this dream.

8

The Joy of Karma Yōga

Bri. Arpitāmṛta Caitanyā

The coronavirus struck terror in the hearts of people all over the world. It also dealt a blow to our collective ego. Put together, all the coronaviruses weigh only 2.5 grams! That was all it took to subjugate the world.

At times like these, people turn to God or the Guru for shelter and guidance. That's exactly what Arjuna did thousands of years ago. He told Kṛṣṇa, "I have taken refuge in you. Instruct me!" (*Bhagavad Gītā*, 2.7). Kṛṣṇa was Arjuna's close friend. But it was only after he looked upon the Lord as his Guru and took refuge in him that Arjuna became worthy of receiving divine teachings. Similarly, what matters is not whether we are physically with Amma but with what attitude we call out to her.

The *Bhagavad Gītā* (Song of God) has been sung incessantly over the past five millennia, nurturing the political, social and cultural lives of millions. It was not intended for Arjuna alone. If it was, it would not have resonated worldwide. The message of the *Gītā* is universal. Lord Kṛṣṇa made Arjuna an instrument to impart his message to the world.

Mahātmās (spiritually illumined souls) have been born in every era in Bhārat (India) to restore dharma and to reveal the wisdom of the Vēdas. These sages interpret the ancient teachings according to the needs of the time and place. Society is now in dire straits. Selfless love and sacrifice seem to have vanished. People now prioritize worldly pleasures over everything else. Many among the younger generation are addicted to drugs and drinking. Amma has incarnated to spread the light of love and compassion. She is not only a treasure to India but an inspiration to the world also.

I saw Amma for the first time on November 12th, 1991. From that day onwards, I wanted to become a resident of the Amṛtapuri Āśram. I had to wait three years. In the meantime, I went to Amma's Kozhikode Āśram every Sunday for bhajans. My family disapproved of my worshipping Amma. They even rebuked me for going to the āśram. But still, I would go. Their disapproval made me feel closer to Amma. I had to travel for over an hour to reach the āśram and had to leave before the bhajans ended. I would catch the 5:30 p.m. bus to reach home by 6:45 p.m.

One day, the bus arrived very late, at 6:55 p.m. By the time I reached my destination, it was dark. I had to cross a bridge over a river to reach home. There was a thick forest on either side of the river. As I approached the middle of the bridge, I saw two thugs sitting there, talking and smoking. I recognized them; they had molested many women in the area before. I felt like a lamb walking towards wolves. I prayed to Amma and walked quickly. When the men saw me passing by, they got up and started following me. I mentally called out to Amma in desperation and started running in a panic. They yelled, "Stop! Don't go alone in the dark. We will come with you."

I shouted back, "No! My Mother is with me to guide and protect me." I began crying out, "*Rakṣikka vēṇḍum ammā!*" ("O Mother, protect me!"), lines from the bhajan '*Ammā Ammā Tāyē.*'

A bright moon lit my way. The thugs were unable to catch up as the path was strewn with rocks and stones. Thus, Amma protected me and guided me home safely.

Often, our actions are motivated by our nature, as Kṛṣṇa says:

> *na hi kaścit kṣaṇam api jātu tiṣṭhatyakarma-kṛt*
> *kāryatē hyavaśaḥ karma sarvaḥ prakṛtijair-guṇaiḥ*
> None can remain without action for even a moment. In fact, all beings are helplessly compelled to act by their innate qualities. (3.5)

Our actions reflect our *guṇas* (tendencies or attributes): *sattva* (goodness), *rajas* (passion), and *tamas* (dullness or ignorance). Our *karma* (action) varies according to the interplay of the guṇas. These tendencies propel us to act in certain ways. Hence, it is impossible to give up karma. This is also why human beings alone act against nature. All other beings instinctively obey the laws of nature. For example, when a cow eats grass, it never pulls it out by the root. Even if they are dying of starvation, cows will never eat meat. Similarly, a lion never eats grass. Unlike animals, human beings are blessed with the faculty of discernment. This is why we are subject to the laws of morality.

The difference between our actions and Amma's is that ours are prompted by our *prārabdha* (fate) whereas Amma acts purely out of her will, concerned only with the welfare of the world.

Lord Kṛṣṇa says as much:

> *na mē pārthāsti kartavyam triṣu lokēṣu kiñcana*
> *nānavāptam avāptavyam varta ēva ca karmaṇi*
> O Arjuna, I have no duty to discharge at all. I have nothing to gain or accomplish. Yet, I immerse myself in work. (3.22)

To appreciate this verse, we need only observe Amma. She does not remain idle for even a moment. Even when the pandemic restricted the number of hours she could spend giving darśan, Amma remained busy. In fact, she had even more work than before because of the turmoil in the world.

But no matter how much work they do, mahātmās have no sense of being a doer. They remain detached from their actions, like butter floating on water.

Once, Śrī Kṛṣṇa asked the *gōpīs* (milkmaids) to take some food to Sage Durvāsa, who lived on the other side of the Yamunā River. The gōpīs prepared a feast and set off, but found the river turbulent. When the gōpīs asked Kṛṣṇa what to do, he said, "Tell the Yamunā that if Śrī Kṛṣṇa is an *akhaṇḍa brahmacārī* (perfectly celibate), she should part for you."

The gōpīs did as they were told, and the Yamunā parted immediately. The gōpīs went to Durvāsa, who partook of everything they had prepared. The gōpīs were pleased that the sage appreciated their cooking and were gratified to see his robust appetite. After the sage had eaten, the gōpīs sought his advice on how to cross the Yamunā. Durvāsa said, "Tell the Yamunā that if Durvāsa has not eaten anything today, she should part for you."

Once again, the gōpīs did as they were told, and the river parted. The meaning of this story is that mahātmās do not identify with any action they do. They act with perfect detachment.

Amma says, "Children, a play performed on stage evokes different emotions in those watching. The audience might laugh or cry along with the actors. But the playwright will not be affected. He knows what is going to happen next. Mahātmās are like this. They know what is happening now and what will happen later. One may ask, why do they bother to perform any action at all? It is to set an example for us, to help us cultivate an awareness of *dharma* (duty)."

Lord Kṛṣṇa explains this in the *Bhagavad Gītā:*

> *yadyad ācarati śrēṣṭhaḥ tattat ēvētarō janaḥ*
> *sa yatpramāṇam kurutē lōkaḥ tad anuvartatē*
> Whatever actions great people do, the masses will emulate.
> The world will strive to rise up to the standards they set. (3.21)

For people like us, with egos and attachments, spiritual masters prescribe *karma yōga*—the practice of using karma as a means to attain God. If we do our karma as an offering to God, it will bring peace and happiness to ourselves and to others. When a honeybee flies from flower to flower, collecting honey, it enjoys the nectar. In the same way, when our actions are motivated by love for Amma, they become sweet experiences for us.

I have always been afraid of death. Seeing a dead body would terrify me. Because of that, I never visited a place where death had occurred, even if it was a relative's or neighbor's house. I could not bring myself to go to the ground where my father had been cremated, even two years after he died.

But when I became an āśram resident, the first *sēvā* (selfless service) assigned me was at the Amritakripa Hospice in Mumbai. Sometimes, after a patient has died, relatives will not come to claim the body. If the death took place at night, we would keep the body in the mortuary and take it to the cremation ground the next day. Thus, Amma made me face what I had tried to avoid all my life and helped me overcome my fears. By her grace, I was able to do my sēvā with love.

Amma says, "There is no point in performing actions mindlessly, like a machine. Only when we act with alertness and intelligence will our actions benefit the world."

Once, I was traveling by bus to Shuranad to conduct *Gītā* classes there for some children. As the bus was crowded, I was standing. With one hand, I was holding the grab handle, and with the other, I was clutching a ₹100 note. Suddenly, the note flew out of my hand. My heart skipped a beat, thinking that I had lost Amma's money because of my carelessness. I told the driver what had happened. He stopped the bus and the bus cleaner and I started searching for it, but we did not find the note. I recalled Amma's words, that it hurts her more when her children act carelessly than when we lose money.

On my way back, while waiting for the bus at Karunagapally, I saw the bus cleaner running to me. He said, "Sister, we found your money! When we reach Parayakadavu, I will get the money from the driver."

I was so relieved to hear this! When the driver saw me, he passed me ₹100. I asked him, "How did you find this?"

He explained that a woman wearing a white sari gave him the money. Usually, nobody from the āśram other than me goes to Shuranad. I wondered who this woman in white might be.

Even though we are all engaged in karma, not all of us are engaged in karma yōga. Karma done with a sense of ego and a desire for the fruit of action is not yōga. Only karma performed without any vested interest and as an offering to God is yōga. Only karma yōga can purify the mind. Lord Kṛṣṇa has given karma yōga another beautiful name: *yajña* or sacrifice.

Amma says that the *yuddha* (war) Arjuna fought became a yajña, whereas the yajña that Dakṣa performed led to a yuddha. Arjuna had surrendered his ego to Lord Kṛṣṇa. This elevated even something as intrinsically dreadful as war into a noble sacrifice. But Dakṣa degraded what was supposed to be a yajña into a yuddha because of his pride and resentment towards God.

Once, a man was resting by the side of the road. A friend walking by asked him, "Why are you just sitting there?"

The man said, "I'm not just sitting. I'm breathing."

Perhaps he was joking, but there is a great truth hidden in his words. No one can live without being engaged in some action or the other, even for a second. All actions, whether physical, mental or verbal, are karma.

In spirituality, what matters more than what we do is the attitude behind each action. I remember a story that Amma tells. Some sculptors were chiseling stone to make idols. A traveler asked one of them what he was doing. He answered angrily, "Can't you see? I'm chipping away at a stone!" The traveler asked the same question to another sculptor, who dropped his chisel and said dejectedly, "I'm trying to earn a livelihood." The man approached a third sculptor and asked the same question. This sculptor smiled and said, "I am carving an idol."

All three men were doing the same karma, but their attitudes were different. The first sculptor saw his work as drudgery. The second sculptor saw it as a means to earn a living. The third sculptor saw his work as a devotional experience, anticipating the idol in the stone.

We can learn to transform any karma into karma yōga. Amma's life is the best example of how she turned every occasion into an opportunity to worship. She performs both visible and invisible karma. Amma says that she is a sweeper who clears the garbage in our minds. Amma does not observe office hours. She works day in and day out, without complaint, to uplift her children.

May we all be able to perform all our actions with joy, alertness and awareness.

9
Love For All Beings

Br. Mitrāmṛta Caitanya

When I first visited Amṛtapuri in 1996, I did not accept Amma as a Guru, or at least not as *my* Guru. It was not because I did not recognize her greatness; nor was it because I had another Guru. I just foolishly imagined that I did not need a Guru.

I came to the āśram on an Enfield motorbike, wearing a black leather jacket and jeans. I had long hair and arrived with a group of people. No, it was not a rock band or heavy metal group. My meditation teacher was leading a four-month, all-India pilgrimage on motorbikes. After visiting Amṛtapuri, my friends continued their pilgrimage but mine ended here. I sold my bike, having found in Amma an embodiment of true and unconditional love. I met someone who expresses divine love for God by embracing everybody. My experience of Amma was supremely touching, impressive and unbelievable.

My journey through India had been inspiring. I had read a lot about unconditional love from saints of different religious traditions. All of them agreed that we have this love within us. I was yearning to experience it. I thought that all I needed to do was to meditate enough to find this kind of love. I believed that I could do so without a Guru.

Then, for the first time, I met someone who not only talks about love, but who is love incarnate. I decided to come to Amṛtapuri every year for a few months at a time to learn from Amma. But in my ignorance, I had accepted her merely as a teacher, just as I had accepted my yōga teacher in Mysore or my Tai Chi teacher in Malaysia. Little did I know that if I really want to learn about unconditional love, I must surrender to her fully; I must practice what she teaches and rid myself of impurities, which prevent me from seeing everything in creation with an equal eye. The scriptures not only praise the Guru, they also clearly explain the importance and role of the Guru. Reading the scriptures over the years, I slowly started to understand that we do need a Guru to progress spiritually.

The spiritual journey is about transcending our limited sense of 'I.' How can the 'I,' who thought itself self-sufficient, ever transcend itself? It is not possible without total surrender to the master. Learning to surrender is itself humbling. Even preparing this talk taught me one humbling lesson after another. I had to accommodate changes to the topic, time and date. But as Amma often says, even contemplating a spiritual topic and preparing for the discourse based on it, are forms of satsaṅg.

My subject is love or non-hatred towards all beings. There are two beautiful verses on this subject in Chapter 12 of the *Bhagavad Gītā*. Unlike worldly love, which often starts with 'love' but ends in hatred, this sacred teaching starts with *advēṣa* (non-hatred) and ends with *prīti* (love):

advēṣṭā sarva-bhūtānām maitraḥ karuṇa ēva ca
nirmamō nirahaṅkāraḥ sama-duḥkha-sukhaḥ kṣamī
santuṣṭaḥ satatam yōgī yatātmā dṛḍhaniścayaḥ
mayyarpita-manō-buddhir-yō mad-bhaktaḥ sa mē priyaḥ

> That devotee who is free from malice towards all living beings; who is friendly and compassionate towards all; who is detached from feelings of 'I' and 'mine;' who remains equipoised in sorrow and happiness; who is forgiving; who is ever-content; who is steady in meditation; and who is self-controlled, firm in conviction, and dedicated to me in mind and intellect; such a devotee is dear to me. (13 – 14)

The chapter in which these verses appear is entitled *Bhakti Yōga*, the path of devotion. In the last eight verses of this chapter, Lord Kṛṣṇa lists the specific qualities of the *parābhakta* (supreme devotee). The verses quoted earlier are the first two of these eight verses, collectively known as *Amṛtāṣṭakam*. *Aṣṭa* means eight and *amṛta* is the nectar of immortality.

These eight verses—like the verses on the *sthitaprajña* (one with steady wisdom) in the second chapter and the *guṇātīta* (one who has transcended the attributes of nature) in the fourteenth chapter of the *Bhagavad Gītā*—illustrate the characteristics of one who has become firmly established in *ātma-jñāna* (Self-knowledge). According to Ādi Śaṅkarācārya, these hallmarks are mentioned not only to help us ascertain if someone is a *jñānī* (enlightened being). We are to practice the qualities outlined in *Amṛtāṣṭakam*, and taught by Kṛṣṇa to Arjuna (and therefore to all seekers), if we wish to scale the heights of devotion.

Although we can read about these ideals in the *Bhagavad Gītā*, only a Guru can help us fructify them in our lives. Amma recommends spiritual disciplines that can help us cultivate these qualities. She also devises situations that will help us develop an awareness of our shortcomings, and creates opportunities to develop devotional qualities.

My previous name was Dayalu, which means 'kind person.' As it was a name given by Amma, I understood that I needed to develop the quality of kindness. Every morning after my meditation, I would make a commitment to practice kindness when dealing with guests and āśram residents during my sēvā at the International Office. I failed many times, including most recently, when someone came to me to change his room for the fourth time! On the rare days I managed to be friendly to everyone I served, I might have forgotten to be kind to my colleagues. Although we might not always be able to follow Amma's instruction to be kind to others, it is important to set the intention each day. Only if we commit ourselves to practicing kindness can we become aware of the limitations that prevent us from expressing it.

In the verses above, *advēṣṭa* means free from malice. One who practices and perfects this quality of not hating will have pure love for all beings. Amma reframes the same point by saying that if we cannot love everyone, we should at least try not to hate anyone. She knows that if we put in the effort to desist from hating, we can evolve, step by step, towards supreme love.

The verses close with *'yō mad-bhakta sa mē priyaḥ'* — 'Such a devotee is dear to me.' We could rephrase Kṛṣṇa's words: 'Such a devotee truly loves me.' It is not that God needs our love; it means that a real devotee is not someone who expresses love for the Lord only though *pūjās* or other devotional practices but is able to love everyone because she sees the Lord in all beings. Amma exemplifies the spirit of *'advēṣṭa sarva bhūtānām'* perfectly through her darśan, when she lovingly embraces all those who come to her every day. She also creates situations to help us evolve towards this elevated state.

We might wonder, "Why should I love someone I don't like or don't even know?" According to Advaita Vēdānta, the philosophy of non-duality, we are all one, though we have yet to experience this. In the White Flowers of Peace Meditation, Amma asks us to visualize a beautiful shower of white flowers from the sky. This creates a feeling of peace and love within. Then we are asked to visualize them falling on the entire earth. Does this not include our noisy neighbor or the person who grabbed the space we had reserved for bhajans?

Amma tells us to visualize the flowers falling on the *entire* earth. She does not say that the flowers are to fall on human beings alone. If she did, we might imagine holding umbrellas above our not-so-favorite people! By including the entire earth, Amma engages us in a benevolent act towards all. By asking us to shower the flowers of peace, we shower our enemies as well as friends. This meditation is a precious gift from Amma. If we practice it wholeheartedly, not only will the world benefit; the practice will also change our attitude towards all, even our so-called enemies. In truth, we have no enemy. We created them in our mind by labeling them as such.

The next two qualities mentioned in the verses — *maitraḥ* (friendly) and *karuṇā* (compassion) — also relate to *sarva bhūtānām* (toward all living beings). What does friendliness really mean? Does it mean making as many friends as possible on Facebook? No, it means learning to be friendly in all our interactions. Amma says that we must express compassion in our actions; only then can we alleviate the sufferings of others.

She also says that we must act with *vivēka* (discernment) and right knowledge. Otherwise, our actions might not help others.

Just as a mother has tremendous compassion for her child, Amma has compassion for all beings, whom she sees as her children. Whereas an ordinary mother's compassion is tainted by worry, Amma's compassion is steeped in farsightedness.

Many years ago, I witnessed an incident that had a big impact on me. In those days, there was no bridge connecting Amma's room to the Kālī Temple. To return to her room after darśan, Amma would come down a spiral staircase from the temple. Late one evening, a few of us were standing under a coconut tree near the *kuṭil* (hut) to see her coming down. When I saw Amma at the top of the stairs, I thought, "Poor Amma, she looks so tired!"

Amma suddenly looked up, pointed to a frond that was about to fall, and told us, "Be careful." The same, tired face was radiating motherly affection and concern. Even though Amma had just finished a long darśan session, she still put our needs first. In contrast, we are more concerned about ourselves. If I were at the end of a mentally and physically demanding 12-hour shift and hadn't moved from my workplace even an inch, I would be intent only on returning to my room as fast as possible, to eat and sleep.

The next qualities discussed in the verse are *nirmama* and *nirahaṅkāra*. Nirmama means to be free from attachment to possessions or the sense of ownership, and nirahaṅkāra means to be free from the ego. *'Mamakāra'* is another word for self-interest. The word reminds me of the big mamas (mothers) in my home country, Italy. Those sweet, loving mamas have big hearts. If you were their guest, they would be very welcoming. They would lovingly feed you and make you feel at home. But if a stranger selling his goods from door to door asks for a glass of water, they might refuse because he is "not one of us." This is not a criticism of the mamas; they have just been conditioned to be skeptical and careful of strangers. This example highlights the limitations of worldly love. Amma says there will always be some selfishness in worldly love.

Amma's heart is wide open, embracing the whole of humanity. She says that *samatva* (equal consideration towards all) is the hallmark of a true *advaitī* (non-dualist). Samatva means seeing everybody as equal and therefore, loving everybody equally.

My own mother is tiny, about the same height as Amma. My father used to scold her, "You always think about others. Think about yourself!" Although my father has a good heart, he is conditioned by the values of the world. In the West, it is common for us to be taught to look after ourselves first. Self-sacrifice is not encouraged. Amma shows us that a noble life of self-sacrifice is not only possible but the most fulfilling.

A crucial message in this verse is *sama duḥkha sukha* — being equanimous in pleasure and pain. Amma herself talks about samatva being a sign of a true advaitī.

The last word of that verse is *kṣamī*, forgiving. Instead of talking about forgiveness, I want to ask you to forgive all my mistakes.

In order to love everybody equally, we need the Guru's grace. May Amma bestow this understanding of unity on us so that we may ascend the heights of supreme devotion.

10

Hṛdayanivāsinī

Bri. Namratāmṛta Caitanyā

Life was humdrum until I met Amma in 1987. My father's friend, a devotee, visited our house with a locket featuring a photo of Amma and an audio cassette of her bhajans. It was the first time we were hearing about her and seeing her photo. He told us that Amma was a saint and that she had an āśram in Kerala. As Amma was visiting Mumbai, he wanted to conduct Amma's program in a nearby temple, where my father was a committee member, and asked us if we would help. As we were a religious family, his request appealed to us, as it would be an opportunity to meet a saint and serve her. My father agreed.

The plan was to conduct a *viḷakku pūjā*[5] in the morning. After that, we would host lunch for all the devotees. Amma would also briefly stay at our place after the morning program. The temple would host another program in the evening, after which food would be served at another devotee's house.

Although we did not participate in the pūjā or go for darśan, we did have a glimpse of Amma sitting on the stage and leading

---

5 *A form of worship in which the lighted lamp is seen as a symbol of divinity.*

the pūjā. Amma seemed to overshadow everyone else by her mere presence. This impressed me deeply.

Although we had agreed to prepare lunch, we did not know how many people would turn up. We prepared food for about 100 devotees. We started serving food when Amma's darśan started. As devotees were continuing to stream into our house even after darśan ended, the organizers decided that it would be better for Amma to stay at another house. When she heard this, my mother felt disappointed. My father asked the brahmacārī in charge of the arrangements when Amma could visit our home. The brahmacārī sternly replied, "Do you know who you're talking about? Amma is the Divine Mother, the Almighty. None of us have the liberty to ask her when she will come. Our duty is to remain ever ready and to wait patiently." At that time, we did not appreciate the depth of his words.

By the time the devotees left, it was evening. As we had not attended the morning program, we decided to attend the evening program and have Amma's darśan after that. We had not stopped to consider how practical it would be for the other devotee to prepare and serve the evening meal, given that Amma was resting in his apartment. In no time at all, we found ourselves entrusted with the responsibility of arranging dinner as well for the devotees! We had no choice but to forgo bhajans and darśan, and engage in *sēvā* (selfless service) yet again.

By the time everyone had their evening meal, it was late at night and we were exhausted. That was when we were told that Amma was coming to our home. The house was a total mess! As we rushed to clean up, my mother went to the kitchen to prepare food. We imagined that only Amma and a few others would come, but when she arrived, she was followed by a small crowd. We could not even get close to her. Somehow, my father garlanded Amma. Amma poured water over her own feet and went directly to the pūjā room, performed pūjā and sang bhajans. Before we knew it, Amma's house visit ended. My mother saw a white figure dart in and out of the pūjā room. Only then did she register that Amma was in the house! Earlier, we had been told that Amma would stay but she did not. My mother was heartbroken and started crying silently.

In the meantime, Amma, who had reached the front door, suddenly turned around and walked to the kitchen. She took my mother's hands and asked, "Daughter, are you upset?" She ate an uncooked rice dumpling and then took my mother to the pūjā room. She then called the rest of the family and gave us darśan. She told the others, "They are my children!" Her words did not make any sense to us at that time.[6]

We thus received our first darśan in our home. What a blessing! Amma had given us the opportunity to serve her devotees first. No doubt, serving them had drawn her grace. Looking back, we wonder how we had been able to cook for so many people and serve them in such a small space. The memory of it still brings tears of gratitude and reverence.

* * *

In the *Bhagavad Gītā*, Lord Kṛṣṇa says,

na hi kaścit-kṣaṇam api jātu tiṣṭhatyakarma-kṛt
kāryatē hyavaśaḥ karma sarvaḥ prakṛtijair-guṇaiḥ

---

6 My sister joined the āśram in 1993. My parents and I followed suit soon after.

> No one can remain without action for even a moment. All beings are helplessly compelled to act by their *guṇas* (attributes). (3.5)

Lord Kṛṣṇa says that all beings are impelled to act because such is their nature (*prakṛti*). Prakṛti is constituted of the three guṇas: *rajas*, which inspires movement; *tamas*, which causes inertia; and *sattva*, which maintains harmony between movement and inertia. These three attributes influence the mind and intellect differently. Sattva produces traits that lead one towards God; rajas inspires action; and tamas produces ignorance.

Our individuality is shaped by our *vāsanās* (latent tendencies) and will reflect a preponderance of one of these three qualities. Propelled by the guṇas, actions are sāttvic, rajasic or tāmasic in nature. Although our vāsanās govern us to a large extent, we can exercise discernment and refrain from doing what is unrighteous. The goal is to move towards actions that are sāttvic.

A person whose mind is deluded by egoism, a form of tamas, thinks he is the doer and is bound to the outcome of actions. Hence, he is attached to both his actions as well as their fruits. Such a person is called an *ajñānī*—someone who is ignorant of the spiritual truth. In contrast, a *jñānī*, a knower of the Truth, is fully detached from both. His actions are expressions of his experience of oneness. He acts only out of compassion, whereas we act helplessly because of our *prārabdha* (karmic burden).

Since we cannot live without being active in some way, whether physically, mentally or intellectually, why not harness our tendency to do good to others or to serve them? Amma says that selfless service is the gateway to inner purity, which will eventually lead us to the state of perfection, the state of Self-realization.

Sannyāsa does not mean renouncing actions externally. Even if a man does so, will it put an end to his vāsanās? Will his eyes stop seeing or his ear, hearing? Will he experience no thirst or hunger? Will his desires cease? Will he transcend the states of waking, dream or deep sleep? Will he become free of birth and death? Certainly not. Just as someone sitting in a moving vehicle will automatically move with the vehicle, our guṇas will compel us to act. Even thinking is an activity. One may be physically still, but the mind might be racing. This is rajas at work.

The entire cosmos is an interplay of these three guṇas but the *Ātmā*, or Self, is beyond them. In the *Lalitā Sahasranāma* (1,000 names of the Divine Mother), Dēvī is described as *guṇātīta* (beyond the three guṇas). Jñānīs know that prakṛti can only act through the guṇas by the power of *puruṣa* (pure consciousness). For example, the spokes in a wheel can turn only when the hub is steady. The hub is like the puruṣa, which is unmoving, whereas the spokes are like prakṛti, which is always in a state of flux. Change implies an unchanging substratum.

The wise understand that seeing, hearing, touching and so on are functions of the senses. The Self is distinct from and unaffected by the senses. Amma identifies with the Self and is detached from the senses. She gives darśan for hours together, unaffected by basic bodily requirements. *Mahātmās* (spiritually illumined souls) like Amma are born of their own will, whereas we are trapped in the wheel of birth and death. This is the difference between jñānīs like Amma and ajñānīs like us.

Once, while the Buddha was out begging for alms, he came to a rich farmer's house. Seeing the Buddha, the arrogant farmer started abusing him for begging. The Buddha smiled but did not say a word. His restraint unnerved the farmer, who asked the Buddha how could he be so calm and composed when he was being abused. The Buddha replied, "Suppose you give someone a present and that person does not accept it. What will you do?"

He said, "I'll keep it with me."

The Buddha smilingly told him, "I do not accept your abuses."

Though taken aback by the answer, the farmer did not give in to the Buddha. He argued that one ought to spend time fruitfully. As a farmer, he tills the land, sows seeds, and harvests the crops. As the Buddha was young and energetic, shouldn't he likewise do something productive?

To this, the Buddha replied that he, too, engaged himself like the farmer: he tills the minds of people and sows the seeds of spiritual knowledge in them. However, unlike the farmer who labored for own personal gain, the Buddha acted only for the welfare of others.

This story describes how little we understand mahātmās. By implication, it is only when we start understanding spiritual principles that we begin to understand mahātmās better. An experience I had gave me a glimpse of a mahātmā's glory.

In 2012, Amma sent my sister and me to serve in the Amrita Vidyalayam (school) in Odisha. During our second year of sēvā at school, my sister was admitted to AIMS Hospital for nearly a month with high blood sugar levels. Having accompanied my sister to the hospital, I did not have access to email nor was I taking phone calls; I assumed that the teachers would take care of work-related matters.

During this time, several parents tried to contact me. When they failed to get through, they thought I was deliberately trying to ignore them. They threatened to take legal action against the school and inform the media. I only learned about this later.

I decided to seek Amma's advice. As soon as my sister was discharged, we went to Mumbai, where Amma was conducting programs. I approached Amma and explained the problem. Before I could finish, she told me to go and speak to the parents. That was all; Amma did not say anything further.

When I reached the school, the teachers informed me that the parents had gathered to talk to me. I went to the room where they had gathered, addressed all of their grievances, and invited them to meet me individually if they had further questions or suggestions. There was silence. I could only hear my heart beating.

Praying fervently to Amma for her grace, I then returned to my office and waited for the parents. For 45 minutes, no one came. A man who finally came told me that, like the other parents, he had been angry and apprehensive initially. But as soon as I started speaking, he had felt a sweet fragrance emanating from Amma's photograph, which was right behind me. As this man had never met Amma before, he could not have been familiar with her fragrance. But he felt strongly that the fragrance was coming from Amma's photograph. Then, he heard a strong message resounding within him, "Why worry when you have admitted your child to Amma's school? It is not she who is looking after the school, but Amma who is in charge!"

He confessed that he did not hear me speaking at all but only felt intensely that Amma would look after the school and the students in the most responsible way. He also felt that Amma wanted him to convince the other parents about this. He did so, and they left satisfied. While he was recounting this, tears streamed down his cheeks; my eyes also became moist.

We can never fathom how a mahātmā works. Amma just told me to speak to the parents. I merely obeyed her, and she resolved the situation. As seekers, we must allow God to work through us. To do so, we can start by dedicating all our actions to God. When we can bring devotion to our actions, we will begin to feel like an instrument in the hands of the Divine.

We must also realize that God is not separate from us; He dwells within us all. The following experience illustrates this.

Many years ago, during a program in North India, Amma told the āśram residents who knew Hindi to ask the devotees if they had problems, and if so, to let her know. Seeing this as an opportunity to talk to Amma, I started looking out for anyone who needed help. I came across an elderly gentleman who wanted Amma's guidance on something complicated. I realized it would be difficult for me to translate it into Malayāḷam. I mentally rehearsed the translation before going to Amma. As soon as it was his turn for darśan, I started blabbering to Amma and in sheer nervousness, I mistranslated. Amma said, "That's not what he said!" She then correctly explained to me what he wanted to convey. I was astonished. Amma then gave him some advice, which I translated to him.

This experience was a stark reminder that Amma understands any language, for she is *hṛdaya-nivāsinī*, one who dwells in the heart. Her love and grace have given me the strength to persevere on the spiritual path, as the following two experiences testify.

In August 1995, some of us were doing sand sēvā. I was part of a team of four transporting sand in a hand cart: two in front pulling the cart and two behind, pushing it. I was pushing. As the sand was not evenly distributed in the cart, it began tilting to one side. Suddenly, it fell on my feet, causing excruciating pain! My team mates panicked and called Amma, who was nearby, talking to some devotees. She came immediately.

Before she reached, my sisters managed to pull the cart back into position. My feet were swollen and bleeding. There was no hospital in the āśram then. There was no ice either that we could use to reduce the swelling. As there was a transportation strike in the state, I could not even be taken to a hospital.

Amma washed my wounds with water and caressed my feet. I rested my head on Amma's shoulder and held her. The pain miraculously stopped. Those around me were sympathetic, but I was in seventh heaven, as I was holding Amma close to me. She advised the brahmacāriṇīs to carry me to my room, where I was to take complete bed rest until my wounds healed. Amma asked Dr. Mattakara-*acchan* to check if there was a fracture. There wasn't, not even a hairline fracture. Amma's divine touch thus averted what might have been a major injury.

In May 2017, I developed a chronic urinary tract infection that persisted for six months. When the infection proved unresponsive to antibiotics, Amma asked me to undergo a comprehensive medical examination at AIMS Hospital. There, I was diagnosed with tuberculosis of the lungs, and the infection had spread to the kidneys. Amma, who was on tour, was informed of the situation. She contacted Bri. Bhāvāmṛtājī, who was also at AIMS, and asked her to organize help for me. Despite her own illness, Bhāvāmṛtājī arranged for me to be quarantined in a well-equipped room near the Ayurveda hospital. The brahmacāriṇīs serving at the Ayurveda college arranged nutritious food and organic vegetables needed for my recovery. Though in quarantine, I never felt lonely, as I experienced Amma's love through every person who helped me. My heart overflowed with gratitude towards all of them. I doubt if my own flesh-and-blood relatives would have taken care of me the way my spiritual sisters did.

Amma guided me throughout the course of my treatment. She specified what I should and should not eat, made arrangements for me to get a special soup that would build up my immunity, and organized sēvā that I could do. She also advised me on when and how I could safely return to the āśram. During darśan, Amma often spoke with deep concern about me to my sisters, who would share it with me, knowing that it would make my day.

I followed Amma's advice and recovered fast. Even the doctors were surprised at my speedy recovery. As I could not speak to all my sisters, I called Bhāvāmṛtājī to convey my gratitude. Crying, I told her that I would never be able to repay them for all that they had done. She told me that the only way I could do so was by wholeheartedly helping anyone in need.

We never know what life has in store for us — what pitfalls are on the way or what bridges we must cross. Total obedience to the Guru protects and guides us. We are fortunate to have Amma, who lovingly takes care of all our needs – physical, spiritual and emotional. May we all develop the strength, devotion and faith needed to complete our spiritual journey and become one with Amma.

11

Her Promise

Br. Swaprakāśāmṛta Caitanya

Thirty years ago, I was working in Ernakulam. I was acquainted with Amma but had not thought about joining her āśram yet. Once, I went with my friends to her Kodungalloor program. We reached the āśram the night before the first program so that we could participate in the *arcana* early the next morning. Before going to our accommodation, we decided to eat dinner. Food for devotees was being served in a devotee's house, which was about 100 meters away from the venue. As we were eating in the veranda of the house, suddenly, we saw Amma walking by. Back then, she used to inspect the kitchen and other places the day before the programs. As soon as we saw Amma, we stood up reverentially. She came near us and said, "Children, food is Brahman (the Supreme). You should not get up while you're eating, no matter who comes to see you."

Then turning to me, Amma said, "Son, there is no light on the road (from the āśram to the dining place). Many elderly people are walking in total darkness. Amma is worried that they might fall."

Saying so, Amma left. I immediately kept my food in a container and ran to the āśram. I searched and found some wires and bulbs. As the extension wire was not long enough to cover the whole distance, I asked the people living in houses along the street for help. They gladly allowed me to take an extension from their power supply. With their help, I was able to install lights along the dark road by the time Amma finished her inspection.

Later, I wondered how Amma knew that I was doing electrical work even though it was the first time she had spoken to me. Through this incident, she showed me that she knows everything about me.

After this, I started visiting Amṛtapuri more frequently. One Saturday, after meditation, Amma was giving prasād to the āśram residents. By Amma's grace, I also received prasād from her. I wanted to sit near Amma but a brahmacārī asked me to leave. She looked at me and said, "Stay there, little one!" Her calling me "little one" surprised me. Only my mother used to call me that. This experience, too, strengthened my faith in Amma.

Lord Kṛṣṇa says,

> *ananyāścintayantō mām yē janāḥ paryupāsatē*
> *tēṣām nityābhiyuktānām yōgakṣēmam vahāmyaham*
>
> To those who worship me alone, thinking of no one else, whose minds are constantly absorbed in me, I will provide them what they lack and preserve what they possess. (9.22)

We live in our minds whereas the Guru dwells in the truth. The mind is illusory. The Guru comes down to our mental level to elevate us to the truth. The Guru's guidance varies from person to person, depending on our maturity. But her goal is the same—to help us realize our true nature. Amma once told me, "I will go to any extent to uplift you." She has also said that she is ready to take any number of births to uplift all her children.

However, we should know that only a humble disciple receives the Guru's grace. The hallmark of a true disciple is humility. Only then can he or she truly surrender. We can light an oil lamp only with the flame from another lamp. Similarly, only an enlightened soul can lead another soul to enlightenment. The Guru alone is the ultimate hope for a disciple.

It is not possible to realize God without sacrifice or renunciation. Desires, which are endless, cause endless suffering and, ultimately, our downfall. Only through renunciation can one evade the trap of Māyā (cosmic power of delusion). The motto of Amma's āśram is *'tyāgēnaikē amṛtattvamānaśuḥ'* — 'through sacrifice alone can one attain immortality.' In spiritual life, one's actions should be selfless and for the good of others. Only actions done for the sake of others constitute a sacrifice; only such actions will benefit the world.

For most people, fulfillment means having all their material needs met. From a spiritual viewpoint, fulfillment is feeling the presence of God. Lord Kṛṣṇa has guaranteed that he will bestow both material prosperity and spiritual progress on the devotee who has one-pointed devotion to God. From the experiences of many devotees, we know that Amma is no different. She assures us that if we chant the *Lalitā Sahasranāma* (1,000 names of the Divine Mother) daily with devotion, we will enjoy worldly prosperity and spiritual progress.

Amma often says that her children's happiness is her happiness. Every moment of her life is dedicated to loving and serving others. Her life is a saga of supreme self-sacrifice. Amma says, "I am the servant of servants. Amma does not have a place of her own. Your inner heart is Amma's residing place." She also says, "Remember that Amma will never forsake one who has taken refuge in her."

In the *Rāmāyaṇa*, when Rāvaṇa persecutes his younger brother Vibhīṣaṇa, the latter escapes and takes refuge in Śrī Rāma. Seeing him, Sugrīva (Vāli's younger brother) tells Rāma, "Don't trust him. He is Rāvaṇa's brother."

In response, Śrī Rāma says, "Even if a person takes refuge in me once and surrenders to me, I shall protect him from all dangers. This is my solemn pledge." (Vālmīki *Rāmāyaṇa*, Yuddha Kāṇḍa, 6.18.33)

After Rāvaṇa's death, Lord Rāma hands over Laṅka and all its wealth to Vibhīṣaṇa. He thus makes good on the promise *"yōgakṣēmam vahāmyaham"*—"I shall provide them what they lack and preserve what they possess."

In the *Mahābhārata*, in spite of Lord Kṛṣṇa's best efforts, he could not prevent the war between the Pāṇḍavas and the Kauravas. Duryōdhana and Arjuna went to Dwāraka to solicit Lord Kṛṣṇa's help in the war. When they arrived, they found the Lord sleeping. When he awoke, he first saw Arjuna, seated near his feet, and then he saw Duryōdhana, seated near his head. He told them, "The Kauravas and Pāṇḍavas are the same for me. So, I will not fight or take up arms. I will serve as a charioteer on one side. The other side can have the whole *Nārāyaṇī sēnā* (Lord Kṛṣṇa's army). Choose what you want. As I saw Arjuna first, he can choose first."

Arjuna calmly replied, "O Lord, I only need your presence. It is enough if you come as my charioteer without wielding any weapon."

Hearing this, Duryōdhana was overjoyed. Without any hesitation, he asked for Lord Kṛṣṇa's entire army.

We know that Arjuna made the right choice, because the Pāṇḍavas won the war. What we need is Arjuna's attitude of surrender. He had the faith that the Lord's presence alone was sufficient for victory. Here, too, we can see "yōgakṣēmam vahāmyaham" being fulfilled.

If we surrender to the Divine Mother, she will look after us, just as a mother cat protects her kitten. The mother cat keeps her kittens safe by carrying them in her mouth by the scruff of their necks. The kitten, who is totally helpless, has total faith that its mother will protect it. We need such faith. Surrender is the simplest way to a stress-free life.

Interestingly, "yōgakṣēmam vahāmyaham" is the tag line of a famous Indian insurance company. People buy all kinds of insurance policies: life insurance, automobile insurance, health insurance, travel insurance, house insurance... But what Amma offers is the biggest and best insurance ever possible: the permanent cessation of all sorrow. She says, "The mother who gave birth to you may take care of you in your current birth. However, Amma will take care of you not only in this birth but in your births to come..."

This divine insurance is a guarantee that Amma will lead us to Self-realization. She assures us that if we follow her instructions with enthusiasm and patience, we will reach the goal.

A few years ago, during Amma's North India Tour, after the Ahmedabad program, Amma was scheduled to go to Jaipur and then to Delhi. The Jaipur public program, Delhi public program and the Delhi Brahmasthānam programs had been scheduled consecutively. After the Ahmedabad program, I asked the brahmacāriṇī organizing the Jaipur program to get the necessary electrical work done with the help of local people. I then proceeded to Delhi directly with my team as the Delhi program is usually more crowded and Amma spends a lot more time there meeting devotees and visitors. Unfortunately, there was a workers' strike the day before the Jaipur program, and no local workers or equipment was available. I learned about it only when I reached Delhi. Swāmījī (Swāmī Amṛtaswarūpānanda) instructed me to go to Jaipur with my team at once and to take care of the stage arrangements and electrical works for the program there.

I was in a fix. Firstly, traveling with a truckful of equipment from Delhi to Jaipur is not easy because of the traffic and check-post issues. Secondly, I had less than 24 hours to complete the work, and that, too, without any local help. Not knowing what to do, I prayed earnestly to Amma for help.

Usually, it takes a long time to clear the check-posts between states, more so if we are traveling in a truck heavily laden with equipment. However, a devotee of Amma was waiting at the check-post for us, and with his help, we cleared the check-post in no time at all. What's more, we did not have to pay any toll! It was Amma's grace at work.

When we reached Jaipur town at about 4 p.m., there was a police escort waiting to guide us to the program venue. With the help of the āśram residents and other devotees, the equipment was quickly unloaded from the truck. We immediately started the work of setting up the stage and doing the electrical work. My team members worked continuously without sleep for almost 22 hours. At around 7 a.m. the next day, Swāmī Amṛtātmānanda came to the venue for inspection. At that time, I was using a pulley to pass tea and breakfast to several workers on top of a light tower that was 10 meters high. Seeing this, Swāmī felt bad and told me that I should ask these workers to take a break and have breakfast. I told Swāmī that we had no time for a break. Swāmī said nothing further.

By Amma's grace, all the work was completed three hours before the program began. From this experience, I learned that when we fully surrender to Amma after realizing our limitations, she takes care of everything.

During *Amritavarsham50*, Amma's 50th birthday celebrations, which were held in Ernakulam, my team and I went three weeks earlier to do the necessary electrical work. When we arrived, we found that the generator, effluent treatment plant, water treatment plant and water pumping system were not in working condition, and we had to fix them ourselves. This took a lot of time.

Further, there was the immense task of lighting up the whole stadium, which required a lot of time and resources. As we were already busy, this seemed like an impossible task. The stadium had powerful floodlights, but we were not permitted to use these floodlights. Not knowing what to do, I fervently prayed to Amma.

The very next day, the District Collector and other officials from the Kerala government came to inspect the work. When we informed the Collector about our difficulty in lighting up the whole stadium, the Collector immediately called the Chief Electrical Engineer of the stadium and told him to give us full control of the stadium's electrical substation. Hearing this, we rejoiced. As the floodlights were very powerful, there was no need to put up additional lights. I felt that Amma's grace alone had paved the way for the Collector's visit and his timely help.

The scriptures say that there is no shortcut to realize God. But having Amma, who is the very embodiment of the Supreme, makes the pilgrimage to God faster and sweeter. As Amma says, even though air is everywhere, we feel the coolness of a breeze keenly in the shade of a tree. May we all take refuge in the cool sanctuary of Amma's grace and protection.

12

A Mother Beyond Appearances

Bri. Haripriyāmṛta Caitanyā

In the *Bhagavad Gītā*, Lord Kṛṣṇa says that he created the system of *varṇas*, which traditionally divided society into four 'classes:'

> *cātur-varṇyam mayā sṛṣṭam guṇa-karma-vibhāgaśaḥ*
> *tasya kartāram api mām viddhyakartāram avyayam*
> I created the four categories of occupations based on the attributes and activities of people. Although I created this system, know that I am not a doer and that I am eternal. (4.13)

The *Puruṣa Sūkta* also refers to the cātur-varṇya, assigning the limbs of the *Virāṭ Puruṣa* (cosmic being) to the four varṇas:

> *brāhmaṇō'sya mukham āsīd*
> *bāhū rājanyaḥ kṛtaḥ*
> *uru tadasya yad vaiśyaḥ*
> *padbhyām śūdrō'jāyataḥ*
> His mouth became the Brahmin.
> His arms were made kings.
> His thighs? They were made merchants.
> And from His feet were born servants. (12)

This suggests that the ancient worldview regarded the four varṇas as an integral part of one whole. No varṇa was more important than the other.

Lord Kṛṣṇa says that this division is based on *guṇas* (attributes) and *karma* (activity), i.e. varṇa was determined by one's innate nature and sphere of activity. The three guṇas are *sattva* (goodness), *rajas* (passion) and *tamas* (ignorance). As a brahmin is predominantly sāttvic, he performs *pūjās* (rites of worship) and *hōmas* (fire rituals) and teaches the scriptures. A kṣatriya is predominantly rajasic and assigned the duties of war, statecraft and so on. In a vaiśya, both rajas and tamas are predominant. So, he engages in agriculture and commerce. The śūdra, predominantly tāmasic, is entrusted with serving people from the other three groups.

During the Vēdic age, people were divided according to *kula* (family), *gōtra* (lineage) and *varga* (group). The varṇa system came into being later. In its original form, the varṇa system respected a person's innate nature. For example, four brothers (all sons of the same father) were of different varṇas: Vararuci, a brahmin; Vikramāditya, a kṣatriya; Bhaṭṭi, a vaiśya; and Bhavabhūti, a śūdra. Similarly, in the *Rāmāyaṇa*, we see how three brothers—Rāvaṇa, Vibhīṣaṇa and Kumbhakarṇa—were of predominantly different guṇas: rajas, sattva and tamas respectively.

But by the time of the *Mahābhārata*, the varṇas seems to have devolved into a hereditary caste system. For example, Drōṇācārya was always referred to as a brahmin, though he performed the duties of a kṣatriya. Vidura was respected as a *jñānī* (man of wisdom) and as a man of self-control but always described as a śūdra.

Amma says that dharma is the essence of a thing. For example, the essence of sugar is sweetness. The dharma of a lamp is to provide light. Each organ in the body has its own dharma. For example, the dharma of an eye is to see; of an ear, to hear; and of the heart, to send blood to nourish every cell of the body. When every part performs its function properly, the whole body enjoys good health. Similarly, when each individual observes his or her dharma, there will be harmony in society. Likewise, to maintain road safety, vehicles must obey traffic rules.

Dharma varies according to the place and circumstance. For example, a man's dharma in school might be to teach. When he reaches home, his dharma changes. He has to be a father to his children, a brother to his siblings, and a husband to his wife.

In the *Mahābhārata*, Dhṛtarāṣṭra, the patriarch of the Kaurava clan, sought the advice of Vidura, his minister, on who should become his heir. In the meantime, four people, one from each varṇa, were brought to the court. All four had committed murder. Duryōdhana and Yudhiṣṭhira were present. Vidura first asked Duryōdhana what punishment should be meted out to each one of them. Without any hesitation, the Kaurava prince replied that all of them should be sentenced to death.

The same question was put to Yudhiṣṭhira. The Pāṇḍava prince said that he needed to know under what circumstances the crime was committed and also each convict's *kula* (family). After learning about the background of each of the accused, Yudhiṣṭhira presented his verdict:

> As the śūdra is ignorant, he should be punished lightly with a few lashes. The vaiśya, who is more knowledgeable, deserves a more severe punishment.

> The kṣatriya should be sentenced to death because he is supposed to protect the subjects, not kill them. A Brahmin ought to know the difference between dharma and adharma and lead others on the path of dharma. But I have no right to pronounce a verdict on a Brahmin, who is from a higher kula than I.

Based on these words, Vidura gave the order to let the Brahmin decide his own punishment. This is how kings ruled in old days. Generally speaking, though a man's birth determined his varṇa, his actions were judged on the basis of his guṇas and karma.

The ancients lived a life of spiritual observances. Even material life was rooted in spirituality then. In the *Śrīmad Bhāgavatam,* Prahlāda was born the son of a demon king, Hiraṇyakaśipu. Yet, his *samskāras* (inborn tendencies) made him a great *Brahma-jñānī* (knower of God). In the *Rāmāyaṇa*, the highway robber, Ratnākara, became Sage Vālmīki by the blessings of the seven sages. Vālmīki extolled the greatness of chanting Lord Rāma's name. By chanting that divine name alone, he came to fulfill the destiny indicated by his name, 'Ratnākara' —'wearer of the jewel.' The jewel he adorned himself with was the shining presence of God within.

Nowadays, people have become selfish. There is conflict, violence and antagonism among religions. In Amma's *Aṣṭōttaram* (108 attributes), she is hailed thus: '*Ōm sajātīya vijātīya swīya bhēda nirākṛtē namaḥ*' —'Salutations to Amma, who is devoid of all kinds of differences' (10). She does not belong to any religious denomination. She does not discriminate against people on any basis. The only thing she rejects are such divisions. For her, everyone is a darling child.

This reminds me of a Marathi devotee named Eknath. He decided to conduct a *pitṛ-śrāddha* (feeding ceremony for the departed). After making all the arrangements, he invited orthodox Brahmins to the feast. On the day of the ceremony, he saw a poor family walking past his house. One of the children said, "Mother, I smell food here."

The mother pacified the child, saying, "Son, we cannot eat food here."

Hearing their conversation, Eknath thought, "Aren't they God's children too? Perhaps God has come to me in their guise. I shall feed them first!" He invited the whole family to the feast.

When the Brahmins heard about this, they took offense. They sent him a message that they would not partake of the feast, as he had fed non-Brahmins first. Eknath became sad. A friend consoled him and advised him to offer the food to his *pitṛs* (departed ancestors). Eknath called out to the *pitṛs*. Pleased by Eknath's devotion, faith and compassion towards the poor, the *pitṛ-dēvatās* (deities representing the departed souls) appeared in person, accepted the offering, and blessed Eknath!

The orthodox Brahmins had denounced Eknath's actions because they were ignorant of the true meaning of our rituals. Amma says that showing compassion to the poor and needy is our duty towards God. Amma keeps reminding us that doing our duties without the correct knowledge is akin to pouring milk into a dirty vessel.

The *Lalitā Sahasranāma*, the thousand names of the Divine Mother, describes Her as '*ābrahma-kīṭa-jananī*'—'Mother of all, from Brahma (the Creator) to the lowliest insect' (285). Amma is also the mother of everything in the cosmos: all sentient and insentient beings. The same *caitanya* (consciousness) is inherent in all creation.

When we go to a garden with diverse flowering plants, we enjoy the variegated beauty of the flowers. Honey bees also visit, but only for the nectar. They are not picky about where they get the nectar. Similarly, we should learn to see only the virtues in others and not be concerned about their external appearances or behaviors. When we perform *mānasa-pūjā* (worship through visualization) to Amma, we bathe Amma's feet with honey and pray, "Wherever we are, Amma, please help us remember your holy feet. Just like the bee, may we always sip the honey of remembrance of God."

I am reminded of a couplet by Kabīr, a 15th-century mystic poet and saint:

> *jāti na pūcchō sādhu kī pūcch lījiyē jñān*
> *mōl karō tarvāra kā paṭā rahan dō myān*
>
> When we meet virtuous people, we shouldn't consider their caste or other external signs. We should see only their virtues and respect them. A soldier buying a sword will inspect the strength of the sword and not its sheath.

I had my first darśan in 1986, when I was in pre-university. That darśan took place in a devotee's house in Vaikkom, Udayanapuram. A father and son were in front of me in the darśan line. The father was complaining to Amma that his son was not studying, was getting poor grades, and was keeping bad company.

I was curious about how Amma would respond. She told the son, "Son, whether you are by yourself or in the company of others, you're always alone. When you're sitting for an exam, you are sitting alone in the hall. A bird perched on a dry twig of a tree eats and sleeps. But it knows the twig can snap at any time, and so, is always poised to fly off any time. You should have such concentration while studying."

It was my turn next. Amma embraced me and whispered "*ponnu mōḷē*" ("darling daughter") into my ears. I cannot explain the experience I felt at hearing Amma's voice and words. Even after my darśan, her words continued to resound in my ears and entered deep into my heart. That darśan ended around midnight. Amma and her tour group returned to Amṛtapuri.

On our way back to the Vaikkom Temple, we (my mother, her friend and I) lost our way and started to panic. We prayed fervently to Amma. Suddenly, a Brahmin lad of about 13 appeared from nowhere and asked us where we were going. When we mentioned our destination, he said he was also going to the temple and would take us there.

When we reached the temple, we turned to thank him, but to our astonishment, he had disappeared! We felt that Amma had appeared to us in the guise of that young Brahmin boy. Otherwise, how could a 13-year-old boy be out in the middle of the night? This incident enhanced our devotion to and faith in Amma.

Thereafter, my mother, sister and I started going to the āśram every week for darśan. My father, a devotee of Guruvāyūrappan (a form of Lord Viṣṇu), did not have much faith in Amma initially. So, he never accompanied us to the āśram, but he never stood in our way.

At around that time, my father developed cataracts and started losing his eyesight. When we came for darśan, my mother told Amma about his condition and asked her if she could bring him for darśan. Amma said, "Not now."

When father heard this, he became sad. My sister told him that if he prayed fervently, he would be able to see Amma. Every evening, we used to sit together in the pūjā room for prayers. One day, my father remained meditating there after we left.

After some time, my sister went to the pūjā room to find out why he had not come out. What she saw stunned her: Amma was standing in front of Father! Her fragrance pervaded the entire room. My sister could not believe her eyes. She tried to rouse Father from his meditation so that he could see Amma. But he was immersed deeply in bliss. Tears were flowing from his eyes. My sister bowed down to Amma. By the time she stood up, Amma had disappeared.

Later, my father went to Amṛtapuri and had Amma's darśan. Subsequently, he underwent eye surgery and regained his eyesight.

Father also used to have breathing difficulties. One day, his asthma became so severe that he had to be taken to a hospital. The doctor told us that his condition was critical and that there was a possibility that he might not survive. My sister and I left our mother there and went to the āśram to inform Amma. We told her everything the doctor had said. She lovingly asked for more details of his illness. Amma then closed her eyes and seemed to become absorbed in *samādhi* (absorption in the Supreme) for a while. After a while, she opened her eyes, told us not to worry, and assured us that she would take care of him. We felt relieved and returned to the hospital.

When we got there, we were informed that Father had been discharged! No science will ever be able to explain his sudden recovery. Two lines from one of Amma's bhajans, *'Ammē Bhagavatī Nityakanyē Dēvī,'* come to mind:

> *tān onnum ceyyāte sarvavum ceytīṭunna*
> *dīnadayālō tozhunnēn ninne*
> Prostrations to You, who is ever merciful to the oppressed and who does everything though doing nothing!

By Amma's grace and my parents' approval, I became a brahmacāriṇī in 1994. The first sēvā Amma assigned me was incense stick making. Later, she asked me to serve in the Puthiyakavu Amrita Vidyalayam (school). Now, I am serving in the Manjeri Amrita Vidyalayam. Because of this, Amma refers to me sometimes as 'Manjeri *mōḷ*' ('Manjeri daughter')!

Once, while driving the students back home, the school bus got stuck in the mud, which had become slushy owing to heavy rains. Despite trying his best, the driver could not extricate the bus. I tried arranging for another bus to pick up the children but kept receiving phone calls from anxious parents, some of whom even scolded me. Finally, a minibus picked the children up and took them home safely.

But I was still distraught. I looked at Amma's photo and poured out my feelings of distress to her. At this point, the phone rang again, but I was afraid it would be yet another parent wanting to scold me. Finally, I prayed to Amma to give me the strength to face yet another haranguing and answered the call.

It was Swāminī Mātṛpriyāmṛtajī, who is in charge of the Amrita Vidyalayam schools. She told me that Amma, who was abroad at that time, had called to ask her to tell her Manjeri mōḷ not to worry! I had told no one other than Amma's photo about what had happened. But Amma had heard my prayers instantly.

This incident was yet another instance of her omniscience. It also revealed her concern and eagerness to relieve her children of their distress. These lines from the bhajan *'Ennuḷḷil Minnunna'* come to mind:

> *akaleyāṇeṅkilum kāruṇyavāridhi aṙiyunnu nī ende*
> *sankaṭaṅgaḷ*
> *kanivāl akaṫṫunnu durghaṭaṅgaḷ*
> O Sea of Compassion, even when you are far away, you know my sorrows, and with great kindness, remove my difficulties.

Time and space cannot keep Amma's children away from her. She is *pūrṇa-brahma-swarūpiṇī*, the complete embodiment of the Supreme. The very embodiment of the divine love proclaimed by the scriptures, Amma liberally showers the nectar of motherly love on all beings. May Amma bless us all with that nectar of love and help us become *ātma-swarūpīs* and *prēma-swarūpīs*, the embodiments of the Self and eternal love.

13

A Forest of Austerities

Br. Acyutāmṛta Caitanya

> *ōm punarāsādita śrēṣṭha tapōvipina vṛttayē namaḥ*
> Salutations to Amma, who is reviving the noble forest lifestyle of the venerable sages.

This is the 89th mantra of the *Aṣṭōttara Śata Nāmāvali*, Amma's 108 attributes, composed by the late Ōṭṭūr Uṇṇi Nanpūtirippāḍ, a gem among poets. The mantra conveys how much importance Amma gives to austerities. '*Tapōvipina*' means 'forest of austerities,' an abode where spiritual practices are the way of life. Let us see how Amma has revived this great tradition.

This is also the topic of the 17th verse of the 17th chapter of the *Bhagavad Gītā*:

> *śraddhayā parayā taptam tapas tat trividham naraiḥ*
> *aphalākāṅkṣibhir-yuktaiḥ sāttvikam paricakṣatē*
> Practicing the three-fold austerities (of body, speech and mind) with faith and without longing for their results is a form of refined austerity.

The word '*tapas*' denotes heat—the intensity and fervor with which a seeker yearns for and strives to attain God. Amma's life is one of rigorous austerities. Those who have been around her know that her austerities continue even today and they are unparalleled in their glory. Even in these modern materialistic times, one can practice austerities.

The *Bhagavad Gītā*, Lord Kṛṣṇa's teachings to Arjuna, was imparted on the battlefield. As the two armies stood facing each other, ready to wage war, Arjuna knew that the war could end his life; even Lord Kṛṣṇa did not rule out that possibility. But he reassured Arjuna:

> *hatō vā prāpsyasi swargam*
> If slain, you will go to heaven. (2.37)

Why speak about austerities at such a time? Arjuna wanted to know what would be the lot of his soul if he died fighting. Lord Kṛṣṇa explained that war waged for worldly gains brings *prēyas* (sense pleasures), but when it is waged as an austerity, it brings *śrēyas* — what is good for the soul. Amma has often said that Arjuna was able to turn a *yuddha* (war) into a *yajña* (sacrifice) by following his dharma.

Lord Kṛṣṇa then instructed Arjuna on śrēyas. The 17th chapter of the *Bhagavad Gītā* is known as '*Śraddhā-traya-vibhāga-yōga*' because the Lord explains in this chapter the three kinds of *śraddhā*, based on the three *guṇas* (attributes): *sattva, rajas* and *tamas.*[7]

The Lord says that it is the quality of śraddhā that distinguishes one individual from another. The Sanskrit word 'śraddhā' is difficult to translate into other languages. Even Swāmī Vivēkānanda admitted that he had problems translating this term. We could say that it means surrendering the mind

---

7 *Sāttvic qualities are associated with calmness and wisdom; rajas with activity and restlessness; and tamas with dullness or apathy.*

and intellect. In Malayāḷam, acting with śraddhā means fixing one's mind on what one does.

Among the three guṇas, sattva is closest to the Self. Sattva is pure and untainted, and so, more desirable than the other two guṇas. Rajas is associated with passion and attachment, and tamas alludes to confused notions and misguided actions. Tamas induces laziness, lethargy and sleep.

The quality of a person's diet, sacrifice, austerity, knowledge, action and intelligence depends on which of these three guṇas is dominant in him or her.

As quoted earlier, practicing austerities with ardent faith and without yearning for material rewards is sāttvic.

Austerity can be practiced in three ways, through the three instruments of body, speech and mind. Hence, Lord Kṛṣṇa calls it a three-fold austerity or '*trividhatapas*,' and explains them in verses 14 – 16 of Chapter 17. First, he describes the austerities of the body:

> *dēva-dwija-guru-prājña- pūjanam śaucam ārjavam*
> *brahmacaryam ahimsā ca śārīram tapa ucyatē*
> Worshipping God, the Brahmins, the spiritual master, the wise, and the elders while observing cleanliness, simplicity, celibacy and non-violence is austerity of the body. (14)

How are the above-mentioned beings to be worshipped? In the Vēdas, God was worshipped as Viṣṇu, Śiva, Gaṇapati or any deity the seeker reveres. God can also be worshipped as the elements — e.g. fire, water, air and sun — through *pūjās* (rituals). Mother Nature can be worshipped using her own resources.

In the *Mahābhārata*, Yudhiṣṭhira states that just being born into the Brahmin caste does not make one worthy of being venerated as a Brahmin. One must embody spiritual values. People who exemplify great achievements — whatever be their clan, custom, gender, caste, religion, country, language or attire — are also worthy of reverence. Family elders and teachers, who impart knowledge, must also be revered.

Above all is the Guru, because the Guru imparts the highest wisdom — the knowledge of the Self. Worshipping the Guru is an expression of the heart. Amma often says that in the āśram, there is no Guru or disciple, only a Mother and her children. It is when we become disciples that Amma becomes a Guru.

When Arjuna behaved as a friend towards Lord Kṛṣṇa, the Lord reciprocated that attitude. However, when Arjuna declared, "*Śiṣyastēham*" — "I am your disciple" (2.7), the Lord manifested his Guru *bhāva* (attitude of a Guru) and imparted the highest wisdom.

I have behaved ignorantly towards Amma on countless occasions, not knowing her greatness as a realized master. But Amma tolerated it all. The Guru, who is the very embodiment of knowledge, experiences everything as her Self. It is our sense of duality that is the prime cause of our anger and impatience. But being established in the knowledge that we are all one, it is natural for Amma to have utmost patience. However, to become worthy of her grace, we need to be humble and reverential. We must keep this in mind in every interaction with the Guru. The more respectful our attitude, the more acceptance and reverence we will have, and the more Amma's grace will flow to us.

In 1987, Amma blessed me to stay in the āśram. I could not stay for more than a few months because I did not follow her instructions. As a result, I spent the next 20 years engaged in work and other responsibilities. However, in 2007, I had to discontinue working because of physical illness. I tried applying for every kind of leave, but was issued an ultimatum: either I had to return to work or resign. When I told Amma about my situation, she gracefully let me stay in the āśram, even though I had previously followed my own whims.

Not only did Amma get me out of that desperate situation, she also provided me with an opportunity to contribute to her noble mission. It is only by her grace and compassion that I am sitting in her august presence and speaking to you. I cannot say that I have become a disciple. Nevertheless, I wish to highlight the importance cultivating an attitude of acceptance and surrender to Amma's will.

Another physical austerity that we can practice is cleanliness and purity. Outer purity and cleanliness are stepping stones to inner purity.

Ārjavam refers to what is straight and well-aligned. This includes both actions that are simple and straightforward as well as keeping the body straight. One must avoid unnecessary physical movements.

The next bodily austerity is *brahmacarya*. One whose mind is fixed on Brahman is a brahmacārī. This practice is not possible if the body and mind are engrossed in sense objects. Hence, brahmacarya is a life removed from indulgence in sense pleasures.

Another form of austerity is *ahimsā*, which is the practice of nonviolence. This principle is important but can be challenging to apply in our world, where survival demands that some beings in the food chain be killed. However, it is important to remember that even in seemingly harmless actions such as cleaning or breathing, some harm takes place when we injure microscopic organisms.

Next are the austerities of speech:

> *anudvēgakaram vākyam satyam priyahitam ca yat*
> *svādhyāyābhyasanam caiva vāṅmayam tapa ucyatē*
> Austerity of speech involves using words that do not hurt but which are truthful and beneficial. It also involves reciting the Vēdic scriptures regularly. (17.15)

Speech is a crucial form of communication that enables social life. However, one must be mindful that the words we use can have a significant impact on our relationships and well-being. We can make friends and foes with our tongue!

Amma is known for her exceptional communication skills. Her eloquence is often compared to that of Saraswatī, the Goddess of Learning and the Arts. Amma is able to express herself effectively, whether through elaborate language or simple, concise words.

There was a devout woman who was active in her local āśram. She regularly attended satsaṅg and participated in sēvā activities. She led a happy and fulfilling life. However, her life took a turn for the worse when her husband, whom Amma called '*mōn*' ('son'), fell ill and passed away. The sudden loss caused her to withdraw from social life and āśram activities. She even stopped visiting Amma. She was unable to find joy in anything and isolated herself from everyone, including her daughters and granddaughter. Counseling failed to draw her out of her depressed state, as did the efforts of family, relatives and friends.

After much persuasion, the woman agreed to go to Amṛtapuri for Amma's darśan. As soon as she reached Amma, she broke down in tears and fell into her lap. She cried for a long time before finally looking up at Amma, who gazed deeply into her eyes and asked, "How is mōn?"

Taken aback, she asked, "Amma, don't you know?"

Amma replied calmly but seriously, "Amma knows. Do you?"

These words touched the woman deeply and had a transformative effect on her. They helped her come to terms with the reality of her husband's passing, and she began to live her life as before.

Such is the power of speech. Austerity in speech involves using words concisely and appropriately. We should use words that are truthful, pleasing and beneficial, and not cause offense or distress. We must strive to be civil in our speech. Amma reminds us, "The wounds caused by words are not always visible, but they can be deeper than physical wounds and might never heal. We may forget a positive conversation we had a year ago but are unlikely to forget an insult uttered 25 years ago."

We tend to use hurtful language to others when our mind is agitated. As Amma advises, "It is important to take a moment to stay silent and avoid speaking impulsively. Engaging in practices such as *japa* (repeated chanting of the mantra) or meditation, diverting the mind with other activities like writing or reading, or going for a walk can help to calm the mind."

The verse quoted earlier mentions that our words should not only not cause distress to anyone, they must also be truthful and beneficial to both speaker and listener. Amma points out,

"In some situations, silence is more powerful than words." But sometimes, the truth can be unpleasant. For instance, a doctor may have to give bad news to a patient, but his intent is only to help. In such cases, because the intent is beneficial, unpleasant words are a form of compassion. But few people have the ability to speak the truth when needed.

Our speech reflects our actions. If we cultivate good actions and purify our lives, we are more likely to speak kindly. Amma suggests reading ancient texts daily. Studying and reciting texts such as the *Bhagavad Gītā*, Upaniṣads and the teachings of a Guru can help to purify one's speech.

The last of the three-fold austerities is that of the mind:

> *manaḥ prasādaḥ saumyatvam maunam ātma-vinigrahaḥ*
> *bhāva-saṁśuddhir-ityētat tapō mānasam ucyatē*
> Peacefulness of the mind, kindness, silence, self-control, and purity of purpose — all these are considered austerities of the mind. (17.16)

The key to leading a fulfilling life is attaining peace of mind. This mental state is often reflected in one's facial expressions, particularly in a smiling countenance. Serenity ought to serve as the foundation for all actions. Before embarking on any action, we can meditate to make the mind peaceful. As Amma often instructs, "Come what may, I will remain happy. Happiness is a decision."

The next mental austerity is gentleness. This involves refraining from violence, cruelty, deceit, intolerance and anger in our thoughts and actions. Reflecting on God's qualities of mercy can help us develop gentleness. We should strive to maintain gentleness in our thoughts and actions even when faced with criticism, blame, judgment, sarcasm or contempt. How we interact with others reveals how much we have progressed spiritually. We must be able to uphold the austerities of mind, speech, and body even in difficult situations.

Another mental discipline is silence. This does not necessarily mean refraining from speech; true silence is stilling the mind. This state can be achieved by eliminating our likes and dislikes. To do so, we must contemplate spiritual principles found in the teachings of our Guru or sacred texts such as the *Bhagavad Gītā* and Upaniṣads. Thus, silence is often considered a form of meditation by spiritual masters.

Another form of mental discipline is self-control or mastery of the mind. This practice involves directing one's thoughts to a specific focus and maintaining that focus. When one-pointed, the mind is not easily distracted. Self-control enables one to guide the mind towards what is right.

Having a pure and selfless intention, i.e. purity of purpose, is an aspect of mental discipline. This attitude is reflected in a mind that is free of selfishness and pride, and which is focused only on the well-being of others. A person who practices mental discipline cannot ignore the suffering of others, and instead cultivates a mindset of compassion and concern for the welfare of all beings.

How can we practice this three-fold austerity until it becomes perfect? Lord Kṛṣṇa says that austerities must be practiced with utmost faith and alertness. Even if we encounter obstacles, we must remain unperturbed. A seeker who can sustain his practice of austerities in the forest is admirable, but one who can do so amidst crowds of people is even more commendable.

The legend of King Ambarīṣa is a good example. He practiced the three-fold austerities throughout his life. He had so much devotion to Lord Viṣṇu that the Lord blessed him with one of his signature weapons, the *Sudarśana Cakra*, a lethal, spinning discus.

Ambarīṣa was observing a fast, which had to be broken at a specific time. But his guest, Sage Durvāsa, had gone to bathe and had not returned. The royal priests advised the king to sip a little water to break the fast. This way, the king could avoid violating the protocol of eating before his guest arrived. The king did as he was advised.

When Sage Durvāsa arrived, he became furious when he learned that the king had not waited for him to break his fast. Using the powers gained from his austerities, the sage conjured an apparition and ordered him to attack Ambarīṣa.

The king was a man of deep surrender and ardent faith. The Sudarśana Cakra killed the apparition and began to fly towards Sage Durvāsa. The sage fled to Mount Kailāś, the abode of Lord Śiva, but the Cakra pursued him there. Lord Śiva told Durvāsa that only Lord Viṣṇu could stop the divine weapon. Durvāsa rushed to Lord Viṣṇu. When Durvāsa told the Lord about his plight, the Lord said:

> *jñānam tapaśca vinayānvitamēva mānyam*
> Knowledge and austerities are meaningful only when accompanied by humility. (*Nārāyaṇīyam*, 9.33.8)

Lord Viṣṇu then told Durvāsa to seek forgiveness from King Ambarīṣa. The sage humbly begged the king to forgive him. Ambarīṣa offered prayers to the Sudarśana Cakra and requested it to desist. The sage realized that although King Ambarīṣa had attained immense spiritual power through his austerities, he was humble.

Sāttvic austerities are free from the expectation of results. That is what *'aphalākāṅkṣibhiḥ'* means. If one surrenders fully to the Lord, without any expectation, one attains salvation. The demon kings Hiraṇyakaśipu and Rāvaṇa also practiced severe austerities, but they did so only to fulfill their desires. Such austerities are not sāttvic. Neither the scriptures nor spiritual masters recommend rajasic or tāmasic austerities.

Amma constantly shows us innumerable ways of engaging in sāttvic austerities. Her smiling face, kind words and compassionate actions are a perfect summary of the three-fold austerities. These are the kinds of austerities that earnest spiritual seekers can emulate and thus become befitting of her grace.

14

Surrender

Br. Gaṇēśa Uḍupa

Amma once asked me which my favorite verse in the *Bhagavad Gītā* was. I quoted the following verse:

> *sarva dharmān parityajya mām ēkam śaraṇam vraja*
> *aham tvām sarva pāpēbhyō mōkṣayiṣyāmi mā śucaḥ*
> Abandon all other *dharmas* (duties) and surrender to me alone.
> I shall save you from all sins. Do not grieve. (18.66)

In a sense, this verse is the quintessence of the *Gītā*. It promises *mōkṣa* (spiritual liberation) if we surrender to God or the Guru.

One meaning of 'dharma' is 'righteous duty.' For example, we might have duties as a son, husband and citizen. But there is a *parama-dharma*, a supreme duty: to discover God in ourselves and others. Lord Kṛṣṇa says that if we dedicate ourselves to this goal, he will take full responsibility for any consequence that might arise as a result of our failing to fulfill our lesser duties.

A shining example of surrender to God was Ratnākara, who earned his living and supported his family through plunder and murder. After meeting *the saptarṣis* (seven enlightened sages), who advised him to chant the name of Rāma and to turn over a new leaf, Ratnākaran plunged into *sādhana* (spiritual practice).

In time, he became Vālmīki, the illustrious sage and author of the *Rāmāyaṇa*.

Sage Rāmānuja, the foremost proponent of Viśiṣṭādvaita (qualified non-duality), says, "Any activity that one performs to reach a spiritual goal is dharma." According to legend, Ādi Śaṅkarācārya, who advocated Advaita (non-duality), once encountered an old man mechanically reciting the rules of Sanskrit grammar. Taking pity on him, the sage sang, *"Bhaja gōvindam bhaja gōvindam gōvindam bhaja mūḍhamate"* — "O fool, worship the Lord."

To find God or realize our true nature, we must first surrender to the Guru. I once told Amma that everyone in the āśram had surrendered to her and were hence eligible for mōkṣa. Amma said no one has surrendered to her. To explain what surrender is, she gave the example of devotees in temples. She said that even while praying, their minds are on whether someone might steal the footwear they left outside the temple entrance. "That's not surrender," Amma said. She said that true surrender is surrendering the mind to God in all our activities. This means remembering Him while doing any work and accepting any outcome as a gift from Him.

In order to have surrender to God, Amma suggests cultivating *śraddhā* (attentive faith), *bhakti* (devotion) and *viśwās* (trust). There is not a day when Amma doesn't mention śraddhā. The motto of Amrita Vishwa Vidyapeetham (university) is, *"Śraddhāvan labhatē jñānam"* — "Only one who has śraddhā gains knowledge (of God)." Once we know God, we will love Him. Love will enable us to trust Him. That is when we can surrender fully to God.

Why does God want us to surrender to Him? The truth is that divine consciousness is shining within us, but its light is being obscured by the ego. By relinquishing our ego, the Divine can act through us fully. We then become a conduit for the highest energy. God is omniscient, omnipresent and omnipotent. He does not need anything from us. But we need Him to fulfill our lives.

The *gōpīs* (milkmaids) of Vṛndāvan expressed their devotional condition to Uddhava thus: "We have only one mind, which is with Kṛṣṇa. If we had many minds, then we could have used each one for different purposes."

Spirituality is nothing but gaining that one-pointed mind. This is also what Kṛṣṇa meant when he said, *"mām ēkam śaraṇam vraja"* — "surrender to Me (God) alone." It is not that the gōpīs weren't involved in worldly transactions. They sold dairy products. But Amma said that the gōpīs labeled the milk, yogurt, butter and ghee they sold as Gōvinda, Mādhava, Gōpala, Kēśava and so on. Thus, they maintained the remembrance of God.

Perhaps, the most poignant illustration of complete surrender to the Divine is the episode in which Duśāsana tried to disrobe Draupadī. At first, she was sure that her five husbands would save her, but they averted their eyes. She then thought the elders — Drōṇācārya, Kṛpācārya, Vidura and Bhīṣma — would come to her help. But they, too, failed to act. Draupadī realized that God was her only true refuge. She raised both hands aloft, and called out with all her heart to Lord Kṛṣṇa, who protected her modesty by mysteriously transforming her sari into endless reams of cloth.

Amma often says that to become a hero, we must first become a zero. This is another expression of surrender. I asked her, "How to become a zero?"

Amma said "The ego has to go. Just as rivers merge in the ocean, we must surrender everything to God, without harboring the notion of being a doer or enjoyer." We must strive to align our will with God's.

There is no better role model of how to work without ego than Amma. Though born in a remote corner of the world, she transformed her birthplace into a world-famous spiritual center, which is now the nucleus of an empire of love, compassion and humanitarian works. And yet, she claims nothing.

Lord Kṛṣṇa explains how we can surrender to the Divine:

> *manmanā bhava madbhaktō madyājī mām namaskuru*
> *māmēvaiṣyasi satyam tē pratijānē priyō'si mē*
> Think of me constantly, become my devotee, worship me and pay homage to me.
> Thus, you will definitely come to me. I promise you this because you are dear to me. (18.65)

Amma knows that it is difficult for us to meditate 24 hours a day. So, she advises us to spend our time fruitfully in a range of spiritual practices: *arcana* (reciting the names of God), meditation, *mantra japa* (repeated chanting of a mantra), *sēvā* (selfless service), scriptural study, listening to *satsaṅgs* (discourses on spiritual topics), and singing bhajans.

Amma also advises us to understand the nature of the world. In the bhajan *'Kālī Mahēśwariyē,'* the poet describes the world as *'māyāmayam anityam duḥkhapradam'* — 'illusory, transient and full of sorrow.' When this understanding arises, our worldly cravings will cease: *'ī lōkam vēṇḍa tāyē'*—'O Mother, I don't want this world.' When we have got enough of the world, we will turn to God with an attitude of surrender.

Amma narrates a story from Lord Rāma's life to illustrate this point. Once, while traveling in the Dandaka Forest, the Lord became thirsty. When he came by a river, he put his bow down. A frog on the ground was badly bruised by the bow but it silently bore the pain. The Lord asked the frog, "Why didn't you complain?"

The frog said, "Whenever I'm in trouble, I cry for you, O Rāma. Now, the Lord himself caused me pain. So, to whom should I cry? I don't want to complain. I just prayed for strength to bear the weight of your bow."

Praying for the strength to bear the trials and tribulations of life is an expression of surrender. It is also an expression of devotion. In the bhajan, *'Jananī Tava,'* the poet writes:

> *vēṇḍa puṇyavum pāpavum vēṇḍa ...*
> *ajñānam vēṇḍa vijñānam vēṇḍa ...*
> *vēṇḍa dharmam adharmavum vēṇḍa ...*
> *vēṇḍa kalatravum sampattum vēṇḍa ...*
> *... vēṇḍatuḷḷatu bhakti āṇallō!*
>
> I don't want merits or demerits... ignorance or knowledge... righteousness or unrighteousness... spouse or wealth... What I need is devotion!

What helps us cultivate an attitude of surrender to God is the understanding that we came with nothing and will leave with nothing. Once this attitude takes root in the heart, we won't have a sense of proprietorship.

It has been said that God is especially amused on two occasions: when the doctor says, "I shall save your child!" and when people fight over property. Birth and death are not in our hands. Everything belongs to God.

Some devotees take pride in their 'surrender.' Pride comes before a fall. Instead, we should feel grateful for being able to do sēvā and sādhana, and attribute it to God's or the Guru's grace alone. Such an attitude will keep us grounded.

I once asked Amma if it was necessary to continue doing sādhana after becoming an āśram resident. She asked me if I had discovered her within. This remark puzzled me. I wondered, "How can Amma be inside and outside simultaneously?" Amma then said that if I could see her in all beings, then sādhana was not necessary.

Amma blessed me with an experience that drove home the significance of her words. During one of Amma's US Tours, the tour group stopped for dinner near Lake Erie, one of the five Great Lakes in the U.S. Before Amma alighted from her vehicle, some of us walked towards the lake. I collected a few flat stones from the bank. When Amma alighted, I showed her the stones. She took one and asked me, "Do you see Amma in this stone?" I said no. Amma told me to look again. After examining the stone carefully, I suddenly became aware of the outline of Amma's form. It was similar to the Amma-and-child logo of Amrita TV. Who would have expected to see her image in a stone! I felt that Amma was trying to teach me that the real Amma is omnipresent, residing even in seemingly inert objects.

Surrender culminates in *ātma-sākṣātkāra* (Self-realization). Once, I asked Amma about ātma-sākṣātkāra and why it was so difficult to attain spiritual liberation. My questions were answered when I overheard another devotee asking Amma why she wasn't bestowing Self-realization on her children.

Amma told him to first become dispassionate towards worldly pleasures, give up his bad habits, and sublimate his *vāsanās* (latent tendencies). "Then come to me. Amma will give you Self-realization. Right now, you're attached to your job, wife and children, among other things. Can you really leave everything and come to Amma? Amma does not mean leaving them physically but mentally... Many look for shortcuts or want instant Self-realization. There's no such thing. But it can happen anytime, and you should be prepared. Do your homework first and prepare yourself."

But the man persisted. He asked Amma, "Even demons like Rāvaṇa and Kamsa attain Self-realization. Why not me?"

Amma said, "In God's world, there are no demons. All are good. Everyone is born pure. Gradually, we acquire negative tendencies, develop an ego, and become conditioned. The demonic qualities are within us, but they should go. Rāvaṇa and Kamsa were born to exhaust their vāsanās."

Amma knows everyone's mind intimately. Many have shared their personal experiences of her omniscience. During one US tour, I saw people doing different sēvās, but none could relieve Amma of her work. As soon as this thought arose, Amma turned to me and asked, "Can you give darśan?"

"Not possible," I said, but I thought that I might be able to do so for an hour at most. I knew that all I could do was hug, but Amma's darśan is much more than that. I was also sure no one would come to me for darśan! It is impossible for anyone in the world to give darśan like Amma does. She sees herself and her children as one and does not differentiate between male and female.

I once asked Amma, "Don't you get tired or bored giving darśan for so many hours?"

Amma said, "Where there is love, there is no tiredness." She then asked me if a pregnant woman ever gets tired or bored with carrying her baby for nine months. Amma's darśan is also an expression of complete surrender. Here, it is the Divine Mother surrendering to the needs of her children, and sacrificing herself in the process.

I first met Amma in 1991 in Amṛtapuri. She was giving darśan in a small hut. After giving me darśan, Amma told me to sit near her. She looked at me often and smiled as though she knew me very well. When I expressed my desire to join the āśram, she told me to continue my studies. With her grace, I completed a Ph.D. in Mechanical Engineering at IIT Madras in 1998. After that, I did a post-doctoral fellowship at the Nanyang Technological University in Singapore.

In 2004, with Amma's permission, I became an āśram resident. After a hectic life in Singapore, I was looking forward to a relaxing and pleasant āśram life, doing arcana and meditation, attending scriptural classes, singing bhajans with Amma... I thought I would attain Self-realization quickly. Amma knew, as I now do, that I was not mature enough to renounce many things, including my ego. She sent me to serve in the Amrita University as Head of the Mechanical Engineering department. Despite this, Amma helped me to reduce my ego and desires.

Once, a senior colleague scolded me. Upset, I went to Amma. She smiled and said in English, "Don't be down." Later, Amma said, "I've told you so many times that you are *ātma-swarūpa*, of the nature of the Self, but you are sad because you are identified with your body and mind."

I realized that I had not fully surrendered to her. Amma shows us our weakness and corrects us. I also realized that the person who scolded me helped me reduce my ego. Later, Amma asked him to apologize to me. He did, but asked me why I had reported the matter to Amma. In turn, I apologized for doing so, and thanked him for his help.

I have found that surrendering to Amma yields generous dividends even in my work at the university. She has guided my team through projects such as solar auto-rickshaws, prosthetic robotic hand, and innovative pressure gauge. Amma is an inexhaustible source of amazing innovative ideas.

Once, a Ph.D. student I was mentoring and I submitted a research paper to two international journals, but we did not hear from them even after two years. I went to Amma, explained the matter to her, and said that I would like to submit the paper again to one of two excellent journals. I asked her to choose one of them. Amma told me to send the paper to both the journals. One of my colleagues warned me against doing that, but I followed Amma's advice. One of the journals accepted our paper immediately. The other asked for further revisions. Amma thus saved us a lot of time, and we could improve the quality of the other submission. Because of Amma's grace and guidance, the Ph.D. student was able to publish a dozen papers. He was also blessed to receive his Ph.D. certificate directly from Amma's hand. Similarly, by Amma's grace, I have published more than 100 papers and obtained five patents.

As long as we think we can attain God-realization through our own efforts, we will not. This is nothing but egoism. The

Lord is both the *upāya* (means) and the *upēya* (goal). We should be like a kitten, which is fully surrendered to its mother. The mother takes full responsibility for the welfare of its kitten.

Complete surrender means understanding that nothing is ours. Even our most treasured possessions, the body and mind, are not ours. We did not create them, and one day, they will be taken away. We must learn to accept whatever comes and to surrender our ego to her. This is an expression of pure love and complete trust in Amma. Even though I have not surrendered completely, Amma still accepts me. My prayer is that she makes me intoxicated with devotion to her. To me, surrendering means being completely in love with Amma.

We have all reached Amma, the very incarnation of divine love. Let us strive hard to surrender ourselves at her holy feet and thus fulfill the highest purpose of life.

15

"I am always with you!"

Bri. Sanmayāmṛta Caitanya

When I was a child, I had an unforgettable experience. My parents had gone to Amṛtapuri Āśram, and I was sleeping alone for the first time in my life. In the middle of the night, I woke up with a start. The room was pitch dark and silent. I felt terrible fear and started praying to Amma. From the silence arose the sound of someone walking with anklets outside in the hall. I immediately felt Amma's reassuring presence near me. My fear vanished completely and I was able to sleep peacefully.

The next morning, my mother arrived unexpectedly; she was not supposed to return for a few days. It seems that when she went for darśan, Amma had asked, "Why did you leave your daughter all alone? Go back and bring her to the āśram immediately."

When I was standing in the darśan queue, Amma looked at me and smiled. Her expression conveyed the words, "Daughter, I was with you all along!" That look is indelibly etched in my heart.

The Cherokee Nation has a coming-of-age ritual for boys. A father takes his son to a dense forest far from their tribal village, seats him under a tree and blindfolds him. If the boy can spend the night alone without running back, he will be accepted into the tribe as an adult. But the boy was not to reveal anything about this ritual to the younger boys in his tribe.

Let us imagine what the boy must be feeling as he walks with his father. He sees poisonous snakes and wild animals on his way. When his father leaves him, he is all alone, unable to see anything and wary of what will happen next. He hears the sounds of wild animals nearby and the sudden loud rumble of thunder. Though trembling with fear, he does not remove the blindfold and run away. Each moment seems endless.

Finally, the terrifying night ends. When he feels the warmth of the sun, the boy removes his blindfold. What does he see? Sitting beside him is his father, armed with bow and arrows; he has been protecting him all through the night!

Though we may not always be aware of it, Amma is always with us, protecting us. We will never have to undergo a trial that we cannot overcome or that will push us to abandon our spiritual practice. Also, as seekers, we must not frighten those who are spiritually ignorant; that is why the older boy was not to reveal the ritual to the younger ones.

In the *Bhagavad Gītā*, Lord Kṛṣṇa says,

> *na buddhi-bhēdam janayēd-ajñānam karma-saṅginām*
> *jōṣayēt-sarva-karmāṇi vidvān yuktaḥ samācaran*
>
> The wise should not perturb the minds of the ignorant, who are attached to the fruits of their actions. Instead, by performing their duties well, they should inspire the ignorant to do their duty. (3.26)

This important teaching warns spiritual aspirants not to misdirect their knowledge at spiritually immature people. Ordinary people work in order to receive the fruits of their labor. They earn merit by doing good deeds and incur sin by unrighteous actions. These merits and sins entangle them in a vicious cycle of endless births and deaths. But if we explain this to immature minds, they may get scared and even abandon their duties.

Suppose we tell a person who believes that God can be worshipped only in a temple, "Why are you visiting temples? God pervades the whole universe. You need not go to temples." He may not understand the subtle principle of God's omnipresence, and, confused by our words, may stop visiting temples, thus depriving himself of the peace of mind he used to gain from temple worship. Instead, if he continues to worship at the temple, his understanding may gradually evolve until he is able to see his beloved deity in everything.

The verse from the *Gītā*, quoted earlier, reveals another important principle. How to perform duties in an enlightened manner? In other words, how do we perform actions in a way that will not bind us to the vicious cycle of karma? Once, Swāmī Rāmakṛṣṇānanda asked Amma after a long darśan, "Amma, how is it that you do not look the least bit tired even after embracing thousands of people? How are you able to do the same thing day in and day out?"

Amma simply said, "I do not do anything." The swāmī was reminded of these lines from a bhajan:

> *tān onnum ceyyāte sarvam cheytīḍunna dīnadayālō*
> *tozhunnēn ninne*
>
> I bow down to you, O most merciful one, who does everything without doing anything.

There are many meanings to Amma's simple answer. In saying that she does not do anything, she is implying that there is no doer. Even though Amma is lovingly consoling and advising so many people, she does not feel she is doing anything. This is the best example of renouncing the sense of being the doer while engaged in action. We cannot follow Amma's example of serving the world for 24 hours a day nor do we know how to act without egoism. Nevertheless, if we sincerely do a little bit of *sēvā* (selfless service) daily, our inner impurities will slowly wear away and our ego will gradually weaken.

I will share an experience. Many years ago, there used to be sand sēvā in the āśram every night. Even though I was small, I wanted to participate and I tried my best to work with the shovel, which was taller than me. After some time, I grew tired and could not continue. At that moment, I saw Amma standing right next to me! Surprised, I stood staring at her. Amma took the shovel from my hands and said, "Amma is so pleased! Amma is very happy!"

I realized that what had pleased her was my humble effort. With just those two sentences, Amma instilled the motivation for doing selfless service in my young heart. Even now, when doing any sēvā, I hear the echo of Amma's words. I am reminded of the following mantra from the *Kaivalya Upaniṣad*:

> *na karmaṇā na prajayā dhanēna tyāgēnaikē*
> *amṛtatvamānaśuḥ*
>
> One cannot attain *mōkṣa* (spiritual liberation) through action, progeny or wealth. Only by renunciation can one attain immortality.

Why then does Lord Kṛṣṇa encourage Arjuna to act if one cannot attain mōkṣa through action? Amma also gives a lot of importance to karma yōga, the path of dedicated action. Selfless service purifies the heart. Only one with inner purity can assimilate scriptural principles and experience the light of the Guru's words. Working with others often brings out our latent tendencies, likes and dislikes. The resultant friction helps to smooth out our rough edges.

In the Ayurveda system, patients are not given a curative right away. Their digestive system will first be cleansed so that the medicine can have its full effect. Similarly, knowledge, the sole remedy for ignorance, can only be imparted after the mind is purified. An impure mind cannot imbibe spiritual truths.

The hunger for spiritual knowledge is not appeased so easily. Amma explains this through the following story. Once, a hungry man went to a restaurant and ordered *biryāni.*[8] As he was not full, he ordered French fries. Still hungry, he ordered fruit juice. When even that did not appease him, he ordered a cup of tea and a *vaḍa.*[9] Finally, he felt sated.

What if the man had thought, "I should have had the tea and vaḍa first; then my hunger would have been appeased right away!" It was only because he had eaten the other dishes earlier that tea and vaḍa were able to appease his hunger. Similarly, to understand the scriptures correctly, we must first purify the mind through actions performed with the right attitude.

In *Upadeśa Sāram,* Ramaṇa Maharṣi writes:

> *īśwarārpitam necchayā kṛtam citta śōdhakam mukti-*
> *sādhakam*

---

8 Spicy mixed rice dish.

9 Savory fried snack.

> Work, when done as an offering to the Almighty and without any expectation of its results, helps to purify the mind; this paves the way to spiritual liberation. (3)

Once, a spiritual aspirant approached a scholar and requested him to instruct him on the path to Self-realization. The scholar quoted two *mahāvākyas* (great sayings of the Upaniṣads):

> *tat tvam asi*
> You are That.
> *aham brahmāsmi*
> I am Brahman, the Supreme.

On hearing these sayings, the seeker asked, "Is that it? Only two short sentences?"

"That's all there is to know. If you want more, you must look for a Guru."

The aspirant went in search of a Guru. He found a highly venerated Guru with many disciples. The seeker approached the Guru and asked to be instructed in the principles of Self-realization. The Guru, an enlightened being, could immediately assess the seeker's level of maturity. He said, "I will instruct you on one condition: you must do whatever sēvā I entrust you for 12 years. I will instruct you after that."

The disciple agreed to the condition and joined the āśram. The Guru assigned him the sēvā of clearing the cow dung. Though he did not like this sēvā, the disciple obeyed the Guru and also started cleaning the āśram daily from morning till night. Over time, the disciple became more sincere in his sēvā and started to see it as a form of worship. After 12 years had passed, he approached his Guru, prostrated in all humility, and asked him. "I have fulfilled the condition you stipulated. Could you please enlighten me with the knowledge of the Self?"

The Guru agreed and declared:

tat tvam asi
aham brahmāsmi

They were the very same mahāvākyas that the scholar had quoted years before! But this time, on hearing them, the seeker went into *samādhi* (absorption in the state of superconsciousness). On emerging from it, he asked the Guru, "A scholar had quoted those very scriptural dicta 12 years ago, to no effect. How is it that, on hearing them now, I could experience the Self?"

The Guru replied, "Truth is ever the same. The *Ātmā* (Self) is immutable. The change that took place happened within you. While scooping away the cow dung and cleaning the āśram, you were actually cleansing your mind of its impurities. When you heard the two mahāvākyas this time, your mind was pure and untainted, and thus, the light of knowledge shone within you."

This is the significance of karma yōga. Purity of mind, gained through selfless service, gradually guides us towards Self-realization. Amma herself explained that only a Sadguru knows the precise word or action that will have the right effect on the disciple's mind, and she will use this knowledge to uplift the disciple. One who does not know the disciple's mind will not know how to do this. His advice will not uplift the disciple; it may even have the opposite effect. This is what Lord Kṛṣṇa warns against.

In the early days, people who came to Amma were neither acquainted with the concepts of a Guru or an āśram nor had they studied the scriptures. To them, Amma was just an ordinary village girl, possessed by God during Bhāva darśans. Despite their ignorance, Amma accepted and honored their understanding of God. During Kṛṣṇa bhāva, Amma would put one foot on a low pedestal and stand like this for hours as she gave darśan. Amma's whole body would vibrate with divine energy and her complexion would take on Kṛṣṇa's dark blue hue. Like Kṛṣṇa with the *gōpīs* (milkmaids), Amma would, with mischievous smiles and sidelong glances, engage playfully with the devotees. For instance, when devotees came with grave faces, Amma would keep stuffing their mouths with crushed bananas. Or she would keep on pouring the holy water into their open mouths. At other times, she would remove their glasses and hide them. Mesmerized by her play, the devotees would forget all their sorrows and burst out laughing. To the devotees who wanted to disclose their problems and sorrows, Amma would softly whisper the solutions in their ears. She would impart the courage they needed to face their trials with confidence.

Amma gave me one such experience when I confided my problems to her. She picked up a handful of flowers and instructed me to pray by offering one flower every day for 41 days. When I returned home and counted the flowers, I was dumbfounded to find that there were exactly 41 flowers! This incident increased my faith in Amma, and I gained the courage to face all my problems.

Amma never takes the same approach with everyone. Her methods are based on the need of the person at that particular time of their life. I am reminded of the words in *Amṛtadhāra:*[10]

picha naḍakkunnu niṅgaḷ, amma ottu naḍakkunnu kūḍe

10 A poetical rendition of Amma's teachings.

> *uttamarāyuḷḷa makkaḷē niṅgaḷkku nityatā bōdham vaḷarttān*
> Children, as you are toddling, Amma is walking beside you in order to develop the awareness of the Eternal within you.

My mother Radhamma was diagnosed with a serious heart condition, and doctors had advised her to undergo an operation. She was a teacher at the Chinmaya Mission, where she met Swāmī Vēdānanda Saraswatī, who told her about a *yōginī* in Vallikavu and suggested that they meet her. Swāmī, Radhamma and another teacher went to meet Amma in 1980. As I was just a baby then, my mother did not take me. Radhamma had her first darśan when Amma was in Kṛṣṇa Bhāva. Though she did not tell Amma anything about her heart condition, the all-knowing Amma said, in pure Tamil, "Child, do not worry."

Radhamma felt great love for Amma in Kṛṣṇa Bhāva, but when she saw Amma in Dēvī Bhava, dancing as Kālī with a sword and trident, she felt scared. After that first darśan, our home was often suffused with Amma's fragrance.

As Radhamma's health was deteriorating, she resigned from her job and underwent major heart surgery. The doctors said that she would need another surgery in about five years. True enough, Radhamma started experiencing symptoms of heart trouble after five years. She was told that she would need to replace both valves of her heart immediately. We informed Amma, who firmly said, "No need to do any such thing. Daughter, just remain smiling always."

Radhamma followed her advice. For the next 20 years, she did not take any medication. During this time, my mother moved permanently to Amṛtapuri with us. Amma entrusted her with the sēvā of looking after the children in the Paripally Orphanage. Radhamma is still doing this sēvā.

I first met Amma in 1984 in a devotee's house in Kottayam. I was in fourth grade then. As our family had been doing pūjā to Amma's photo at home every day, meeting Amma was like meeting someone I already knew. Slowly, we started coming to the āśram more frequently. Over time, I began to develop a strong desire to stay in the āśram with Amma. That desire was fulfilled during my summer vacations. Those were the happiest days in my life. I was away from my parents for the first time! In the evenings, when Amma went to the seashore, she would take me along, holding my hand. She would make me sit right next to her during Dēvī Bhava.

I recall an incident that happened when I was in the sixth grade. It was the last Kṛṣṇa bhāva darśan. When I went for darśan, Amma asked me, "What do you want?" I was standing next to Amma, hugging her. I could not answer her immediately. Amma asked me the question thrice. I said, "I want Amma only. That's enough. I don't want anything else."

Amma asked me, "Do you want me?"

I replied, "Yes. I want only you."

Amma asked the same question to another child, who said, "Amma, I want *bhakti* (devotion)." Later, my mother asked me what Amma had told me. When I told her what happened, she said, "Why didn't you ask for bhakti?" Hearing this, I felt sad that I had not been able to think of the right answer.

The next day, when Amma came to give darśan, she looked at me and said, "She is intelligent! She asked for Amma! If one gets Amma, one will get bhakti, *mukti* (liberation) and everything else!"

Those words lifted my heart and dispelled all my doubts. Amma says that if we catch the queen bee, all other bees will follow us. Similarly, if we are able to catch hold of Amma, we need not chase after bhakti or mukti; they will come chasing us. In hindsight, I believe Amma must have blessed me because my family had to go through a very difficult period later, and it was by Amma's grace alone that we were able to prevail.

When I joined the āśram, I was given the sēvā of preparing curry and chutney in the kitchen. The brahmacāriṇī in charge of the kitchen insisted that I do the work alone even though I had never cooked before. On my first day, I was told to make a pot full of chutney. I began praying to Amma fervently while preparing it. It was a Saturday, and in those days, Amma used to give *pāyasam* (pudding) to all the āśram residents in the evening. However, she would serve only a little pāyasam to the diabetics, and would tell them to have something else from the canteen instead. On that day, Amma told a diabetic to have *dōsa* (Indian pancake) and chutney in the canteen. Usually, Amma would have said dōsa and *sāmbār* (spicy lentil and vegetable curry), but on that day, she mentioned chutney, which I had prepared. It might seem insignificant, but for me, Amma's words were an acknowledgment of the chutney I had prepared!

In the *Bhagavad Gītā*, Lord Kṛṣṇa declares that a devotee who takes refuge in him will always be protected. The following incident from the *Mahābhārata* exemplifies this truth. The battlefield of Kurukṣētra, where the Mahābhārata War was fought, was once full of trees. A mother bird had made a nest in one of those trees. The other birds asked her, "How will you protect your chicks during this terrible battle? Look down.

Can't you see enraged elephants, whizzing chariots and fierce warriors? Your nest will be destroyed any time!"

The mother bird replied, "Standing in the midst of this battlefield is my Lord Kṛṣṇa. If it is his will that my chicks die here, no one can save them. But if he determines that my children will live, then nobody can harm them. I have surrendered completely to him. May his will prevail!"

Saying so, the mother bird went to collect food for her chicks. At that moment, an archer missed his target and his arrow hit the branch bearing the nest. The branch and the nest fell to the ground. At the same time, one of Arjuna's arrows hit the large bell hanging around the neck of an elephant. The bell fell right over the nest, protecting the chicks during the raging battle. Lord Kṛṣṇa had protected the chicks because of the mother bird's faith and surrender.

I am reminded of these lines in *Amṛtadhāra*:

> *ammayē āśrayiccu ettunna makkaḷē amma veḍiyukill-ōrkkū*
> Remember that Amma will never abandon the children who repose their faith in her.

May we all keep our faith in Amma, remembering that she is always with us.

16

Amṛta Sparśam

Br. Prasādāmṛta Caitanya

Perfection in life comes when our development is all-rounded. True development is not just physical, mental and intellectual; it is also spiritual and must culminate in Self-realization. We can attain this completeness only when we acknowledge the existence of our fellow beings in creation and act for their welfare as well. The *pañca mahā yajña sādhana* — spiritual practices that encompass five types of sacrifices — is one way to accomplish this:

> *pañca vā ētē mahāyajñās-satati*
> *pratāyantē satati santuṣṭantē*
> *dēvayajña pitṛyajñō bhūtayajñō*
> *manuṣya yajñō brahmayajña iti*
> Five sacrifices must be completed daily: *dēva-yajña*, *pitṛ-yajña*, *bhūta-yajña*, *manuṣya-yajña*, and *brahma-yajña*. (*Taittirīya Āraṇyaka*, 2.10)

These five sacrifices pay homage to five groups of beings:

1. *dēva yajña*: duties towards the gods, and they include *hōmas* (fire sacrifices) and *pūjās* (rites of ceremonial worship), which help to maintain harmony in nature;

2. *pitṛ yajña*: duties towards our ancestors. They include performing pūjās for ancestors and caring for and honoring parents and elders;
3. *bhūta yajña*: duties towards other living (non-human) beings. This involves providing food, care and shelter to them;
4. *manuṣya yajña*: duties towards human beings. This means serving other people, particularly those who are suffering; and
5. *brahma yajña*: duties towards the enlightened. We can fulfill these duties by studying and teaching the scriptures. The knowledge thus acquired is called *ārṣa jñāna* or Vēdic knowledge.

Vēdic knowledge upholds a *dharma* (doctrine of moral living) that envisions the whole universe as a single entity. The ancient *ṛṣis* (seers) of India saw *caitanya* (pure consciousness) pervading all the molecules in creation, and gave this great vision pride of place in life. They shaped traditional daily rituals on the basis of this unitive vision. In this way, the ṛṣis transmitted Vēdic dharma through generations. The practice of these mahā yajñas ensures the survival, security and prosperity of the individual, family, society and the entire world. The following is a brief explanation of these mahā yajñas.

Dēva Yajña

The *Bhagavad Gītā* explains the glory of this practice:

dēvān bhāvayatānēna tē dēvā bhāvayantu vaḥ
parasparam bhāvayantaḥ śrēyaḥ param avāpsyatha

> Pleased by these sacrifices, the *dēvas* (celestial beings or gods) will sustain you. By nourishing one another, you can attain the highest good. (3.11)

The verse enjoins us to perform yajñas and thus please the gods, who will, in turn, bless us. This mutual cooperation leads to the supreme realization of happiness. We can invoke the blessings of the dēvas by doing spiritual practices such as *arcana* (chanting the names of deities, e.g. the *Lalitā Sahasranāma*, the 1,000 names glorifying the Divine Mother), *mantra japa* (repetition of a mantra), and meditation. We must set aside some time for this daily, preferably during *sandhyā* (dawn and dusk) in a conducive space such as a room for worship or any other serene place. We can create an ambience for worship by lighting a lamp during this time.

Pitṛ Yajña

Ancestor worship is given utmost importance in Sanātana Dharma.[11] One who was about to enter the life of a householder would be advised, *"Dēva pitṛ kāryabhyām na pramaditavyam"* — "Do not neglect your duties to the gods and your ancestors" (*Taittirīya Upaniṣad*, 11.2).

We must behave respectfully and lovingly towards the elderly. They must be given the care they need, especially when they are ill or unwell. Touching the feet of parents every morning is a practice that creates in children a feeling of reverence for parents. Special rites such as *bali* and *śrāddha karma*, aimed at propitiating our departed ancestors, must also be performed.

---

11 'Eternal Religion' or 'Eternal Way of Life,' the original or traditional name of Hinduism.

Bhūta Yajña

After worshipping the dēvas and propitiating our ancestors, we are advised to serve other living beings, seeing them as equal in creation.

In the past, a portion of rice cooked daily for the family would be offered to crows. Family members would eat only after feeding the cattle and other household pets. A *raṅgōlī* (floor drawing made from rice flour) would be drawn outside the front door. This would attract insects like ants, who would feed on the rice flour. Caring for animals and preventing cruelty towards them is also a form of bhūta yajña. In the *Bhagavad Gītā*, Lord Kṛṣṇa describes a true devotee thus:

> *advēṣṭā sarva-bhūtānāṁ maitraḥ karuṇa ēva ca*
> ... free from malice, friendly and merciful towards all beings... (12.13)

Bhūta yajña also includes the daily watering of household plants, including sacred plants like the *tulsī* (basil) and *bilva* (Bengal quince).

Manuṣya Yajña

Spiritual masters like Amma consider serving fellow human beings their duty. Dicta such as '*nara sēvā nārāyaṇa sēvā*' and '*mānava sēvā mādhava sēvā*' clearly indicate that serving others is a form of worship. Amma's wide-ranging humanitarian efforts are ideal examples of manuṣya yajña.

Amma's āśram has been at the forefront of relief efforts following natural disasters such as floods, hurricanes, earthquakes and tsunamis. She has provided free homes for those who lost their homes, and free health care, including life-saving surgery, to the needy.

Through the Amrita Vidyalayams and Amrita Vishwa Vidyapeetham — the primary, secondary and tertiary educational institutes that the āśram manages — Amma is molding a generation of youth steeped in age-old values.

Amma asked me to manage the Mysore Āśram and the hospital affiliated with it, and instructed me on how to run the hospital. Initially, we conducted free health camps in the hospital once or twice a month. Over time, we organized free mobile health camps in rural areas and for those affected by the floods in northern Karnataka.

In late 2013, four children from the Salundi village died from dengue fever. We set up a free healthcare and awareness camp in 31 rural areas in three districts. Dr. Prem Nair, Director of AIMS Hospital, sent a telemedicine vehicle along with two final-year medical students from AIMS Medical College. Every day at 8 a.m., the doctors in our hospital, the medical students from AIMS, and others would leave our hospital for the medical camp, and return at 6 p.m. Then, they would pack medicines for the next day. Each day, they traveled 40 – 50 kilometers to and from the campsites.

A devotee from Mysore showed Amma a newspaper report about the medical camps. It was titled *'Amrita Sparsham'* — 'Touch of Amrita.' Amma brought the report to her head in humble acknowledgment. After this, the medical camps became more frequent. We used to struggle hard to conduct three or four medical camps a month. After this, we were able to conduct camps in 31 areas over 31 days.

The health minister, who inaugurated the last medical camp, expressed appreciation for the services that Amma and her āśram rendered. By her blessings, we could serve as humble instruments in her hands and thus carry out this extensive manuṣya yajña.

Seeing our track record, BNPM Ltd., a Mysore-based company that produces paper for the Reserve Bank of India, gifted us a new telemedicine vehicle equipped with state-of-the-art facilities.

Brahma Yajña

The *Chāndōgya Upaniṣad* says, "*yadēva vidyayā karōti śraddhayōpaṇiṣadā tadēva vīryavattaram bhavatīti*" — "Only actions done with true knowledge, with faith in the teachers and the scriptures, and in accordance with the principles of the Upaniṣads, bear fruit" (1.1.10). True knowledge here refers to knowledge of the Self or the Supreme. The ancient sages gave utmost importance to the attainment of such wisdom.

Life in ancient Indian society was divided into four stages. The first, *brahmacarya āśrama* (celibate student life), was dedicated to gaining knowledge. Studying the scriptures and applying spiritual principles to daily life is an important aspect of brahma yajña. Spiritual masters stress the importance of setting aside some time daily for such study and contemplation. The *Taittirīya Upaniṣad* declares, "*Swādhyāyānmā pramadaḥ*" — "Do not neglect the study of scriptures" (1.11.1). The *Sādhana Pañcakam* by Ādi Śaṅkarācārya begins with an injunction to study the Vēdas daily: "*Vēdō nityamadhīyatām.*" It is useful to cultivate the habit of reading (or reciting) any of the following: the words or teachings of the Guru or *mahātmās* (spiritually illumined souls), the Upaniṣads, the *Bhagavad Gītā*, *Rāmāyaṇa* and *Bhāgavatam*. Brahma yajña becomes complete when this becomes part of our daily life and when we share the knowledge gained with others. Scriptural study and spiritual practice will help weaken the ego-based notions of 'I' and 'mine,' thus enabling the flow of divine grace to reach us.

Experiences with Amma

I first saw Amma in March 1991 in Amṛtapuri. I had gone there at the insistence of my sister. Amma was giving Dēvī Bhāva darśan. Seeing her wearing a crown and a resplendent sari, I felt skeptical, but went for darśan at the very end. The moment Amma hugged me, I felt overwhelmed and started crying. I felt as if all the weight in my mind and heart had been lifted and I was fluttering like milkweed in the breeze.

Whenever I recalled Amma's comforting words during that darśan—"Son, don't worry" and "Son, Amma is with you"—I would begin to weep. After two or three more darśans, I was able to quit smoking by Amma's grace.

At that time, I was working in Mysore. After my first darśan, I started visiting Amṛtapuri regularly. In 1992, during a Dēvī Bhāva darśan, I prayed for Amma's blessings to start satsaṅg activities in Mysore. Amma looked pleased and blessed me by showering flowers on my head. For a year, I organized satsaṅgs in the homes of various devotees for two hours every Friday evening. Having heard that I was traveling to these homes on a rented bicycle, a devotee bought me a new bicycle. I began carrying a photo of Amma on the bicycle to the venues of the satsaṅg.

Once, while returning home after a satsaṅg, I decided to visit a devotee who had been admitted to a hospital. I parked the bicycle inside the hospital premises, locked it, and prayed to Amma, "O Amma, I've parked my bicycle here. I will return after seeing the devotee."

During my visit, I started chanting Amma's *Aṣṭōttaram* (108 attributes). At one point, I heard Amma's voice within telling me, "Son, go to your bicycle now! Someone is doing something to it!" I quickly ran to where I had parked my bicycle. When I got there, I saw two men trying to break open my bicycle lock with a rock. The moment they saw me, they fled under the cover of darkness. When I realized that Amma, who had blessed me with the bicycle, had also protected it from being stolen, I was moved to tears.

At work, I would not leave until 7 or 8 p.m., by which time everyone else, including the chairman and director, would have left. But on Fridays, I would leave at 5 p.m. so as to begin the satsaṅg at 6:30 p.m. Seeing my work ethic, the management did not have any complaints, but my colleagues used to make fun of me. One of them asked me, "You keep talking about Amma and organize satsaṅgs and bhajans. Does your Amma know about it? Does she even know your name?"

Hearing this, another colleague mockingly said, "She probably doesn't know anything about this. This is *his* madness."

Hearing these words, I felt hurt and said, "My Amma knows everything. She knows not only my name in this birth but in my previous births as well!"

Later, I thought, "Didn't I just lie to save face?" I recalled that I had asked Amma to bless me to conduct satsaṅg activities in Mysore but had not told her my name.

A few months passed. In April 1994, Amma visited Mysore for the first time during *Viṣu.*[12] For the people of Mysore, this was an auspicious gift. After darśan ended the next day, Amma visited Sai Saraswati Vidyashala (a school and charitable trust); the trust was going to donate two acres of land to Amma's āśram. As part of that committee, I was waiting to receive Amma's darśan. Suddenly, I recalled how I had told my colleagues that Amma knows everything, including my name. When I went for darśan, Amma kept my head in her lap for a long time. Then she raised my head towards her and whispered, "Rāmakṛṣṇayya!" and made a gesture of offering flowers during an arcana. I realized that Amma had just revealed that she knew my name was Rāmakṛṣṇa and that I did the arcana during the satsaṅgs in Mysore. Amma thus removed all my doubts. I joined Amṛtapuri as a brahmacārī in 1996.

A few years ago, the Mysore āśram organized a spiritual retreat at the Venkateswara Temple premises, located on top of a hill, 75 kilometers away from Amma's Mysore āśram. Before the journey started, we prayed to Amma to help us to feel her presence throughout the retreat. Eighty devotees accompanied us. Breakfast for us had been arranged in a temple. While praying there, I received a call from the US. When I answered the call, I heard someone saying, "I'll pass the phone to Amma." But the call got disconnected.

While I waited outside for them to call me back, the temple trustees took me back into the temple. Chandrasekharan, a devotee of Amma and trustee of this temple, asked me if Amma knew about our travel plans. I said, "Of course! Amma knows everything!"

---

12 Festival celebrated by Malayalee Hindus as the New Year.

After breakfast, we set off on the next leg of our journey. When we reached the highway, my phone rang again. I asked for our vehicle to be pulled over to the side. When I answered the phone, I heard Amma's sweet voice saying, "Son, are you all fine?"

I told Amma that all the brahmacārīs from the Mysore Āśram and some of her devotees were going for a spiritual retreat and asked for her blessings. Amma replied, "Okay son, okay. Amma's kisses to my darling son!"

The call was disconnected before I had a chance to reply. Even though Amma was thousands of kilometers away from us, all of us felt her presence. She showed us that, where there is true love, there are no barriers. Truly, Amma is holding our hand and walking along with us at every moment, at each step.

Amma says that when we become a zero, we can become a hero. When we can develop humility, we can perform many good deeds for the world, the way a big water tank supplies water through many pipelines to the needy. To do so, we must allow ourselves to become a humble instrument in Amma's hands.

17

Unveiling Our Potential

Bri. Abhivandyāmṛta Caitanyā

Recently, I read an article by Swāmī Paramātmānanda, in which he recalled a meaningful conversation with Amma:

> Swāmī : Amma, if God is compassionate, why is there so much suffering in the world?
> Amma: Which world?
> Swāmī : This world!
> Amma: You see the world, but as far as I am concerned, there is no world. I see only God.
> Swāmī : That may be true in your case, Amma, and for two or three people like you. What about the millions of people who see the world as real?
> Amma: There is no democracy or majority rule in spirituality. Even if there is only one person who sees the world as a dream and God as real, that is the Truth.

Such is the state of a true yōgī. He has total control over his mind and senses. He does not see any sense objects, only God or Brahman. In Chapter 2 of the *Bhagavad Gītā*, Śrī Kṛṣṇa describes a *sthitaprajña* (person of steady wisdom) thus:

> *yā niśā sarva-bhūtānāṁ tasyāṁ jāgarti samyamī*
> *yasyāṁ jāgrati bhūtāni sā niśā paśyatō munēḥ*

> What is night to ordinary people is like day for one who has realized the Self. What is day to all beings in the world is night to the introspective sage. (2.69)

Ordinary people are blind to the light of the *ātma-jñana* (Self-knowledge). Their ignorance is likened to the darkness of night. But for a yōgī, the Self is like the clear light of day. A worldly person enjoys the sense-objects, whereas a yōgī regards them with perfect detachment. Amma explains it simply: “You see the world, but as far as I am concerned, there is no world. I see only God.”

I am reminded of a story Amma told us. A poor youngster was fishing one day, when, suddenly, there was a commotion. An elephant was charging towards him with a garland on his tusks. Before the young man could run away, the elephant put the garland around his neck. A crowd gathered and cheered happily because the new heir to the throne had just been chosen; that was the aim of the garlanding. In due course, the man became king. He married a princess and lived in the palace happily.

One day, the new king and queen were riding along the cliffs when a storm broke out and their horses slipped. The queen fell on a rock and died instantly, but the king saved himself by grabbing hold of a tree branch. After hauling himself to safety, the king started walking back to the palace but saw neither palace nor kingdom, only his mud-plastered hut with the thatched roof. That was when the poor man realized that he had been dreaming!

It does not matter whether our dreams are joyful or sorrowful. Eventually, we will wake up and realize that our dream experiences were all unreal. Likewise, while living in this world, we walk, eat and work. Once we wake up to the supreme reality, we will dismiss worldly life as a mere dream. Until that truth dawns on us, the world will continue to appear real.

In the past, people were more attuned to higher realities. In Kerala, families used to light the lamp at dusk, as a symbolic gesture of dispelling the darkness of spiritual ignorance. All the members of the family would sit around the lamp and pray. Our grandmothers used to shed tears while chanting the names of God. The elders would impart dharmic values and a noble culture to their children.

These days, many people spend their evenings watching TV instead of praying, and sob over soap operas instead of crying for God. We can learn something from them. Most spectators tend to identify with the actors, and rejoice or suffer as they do, but the director and scriptwriter both remain unaffected. Amma, who is both playwright and director of the drama of the world, is a pure witness to all that is going on.

We live in an age where even children have smartphones or tablets. To many people, these are more important than God. We must learn to turn the mind away from external objects and look inward. The source of all joy is within. We are like the musk deer, searching everywhere for its own fragrance, unaware that the fragrance is emanating from itself. We must try to elevate our mind, which is caught up in worldly affairs, to higher truths.

I am reminded of an experience. One day, I was returning to the Amrita Vidyalayam in Pandalam by bus. When I alighted, there was a heavy rainstorm. All the shops were starting to close because the electricity was out. As I did not have a phone to call anyone from the school to pick me up, I rushed to a shop that was just about to close. I begged the shopkeeper to make a call for me, but his landline was down and he did not have a mobile. Feeling helpless, I started chanting my mantra, calling out to Amma for help.

Suddenly, the shopkeeper pointed to a car in the distance. Someone in the car was calling out to me. It was the school driver and his wife! As Amma says, a mobile phone might not have full-service coverage all the time whereas the mantra's range is constant and infinite!

Amma says, "Today, man is diving deep into the ocean and soaring high into space. We have invented powerful vacuum cleaners that can remove the tiniest specks of dirt but we are not even aware of the need to cleanse our minds."

It is to inspire us to purify our minds that Amma tells us many stories of Rādhā — Rādhā was late in meeting Kṛṣṇa because she stopped to remove a thorn from the foot of a young boy; Rādhā gave away her new clothes to another milkmaid who did not have nice clothes for dancing with the Lord... In Rādhā, we see the perfect devotee, one who always put others before herself and who thus became a byword for inner purity.

Amma is not only helping us cleanse our minds, she is also promoting environmental cleanliness. She initiated the *Amala Bharatam* (Clean India) campaign to make India clean and beautiful, a few years before the Union Government launched the same project under the name *Swachh Bharat*. A Member of Parliament, who came to inaugurate the *Viṣu-tainīṭṭam* program,[13] said that Amma was the one who actually initiated

---

13 *Traditionally, elders gift the young with money during Viṣu, a popular Hindu festival celebrated in Kerala and which coincides with the spring equinox. Amma innovated on this tradition by distributing saplings instead of cash.*

the campaign. Had anyone else initiated the project, he or she would have insisted on being credited for it. But Amma's only interest was sprucing up the country.

Only divine grace can crown our efforts with success. But typically, when things go well, the ego rears its head and we pat ourselves on the back. If something goes wrong and we are blamed, we become despondent. In contrast, a yōgī is always alert but unconcerned about the result of his actions, whether success or failure. Unlike the normal mind, which is like a pendulum swinging between the extremes of joy and sorrow, a yōgī's mind does not vacillate but remains steady.

Through the following lines in *Amṛtadhāra*, the poetic rendition of Amma's teachings, she tells us:

> *ceyyunna karmaṅgaḷ ellām daivam ceyyiccat-āṇennu kaṇḍāl*
> *ceytatu ceytennu tōnnilla, tōnnāykil yōgamāyi tīrunnu karmam*
>
> Once we realize that God is working through us, we will not have the sense of being a doer. Then, *karma* (action) becomes yōga.

To gain that level of mental purity involved in seeing the hand of God in everything, we must cultivate surrender through *śraddhā* (attentiveness), *bhakti* (devotion), and *viśwās* (faith). Surrender happens when we act in accordance with Amma's instructions. While performing each action, we must strive to work sincerely and surrender its outcome to Amma. We must not let our ego get in the way. If we make mistakes, Amma will point them out. If we correct them, we can bring alertness and purity to all our actions.

Amma is a perfect example of *śraddhā* (attentiveness). A Collector[14] who was entrusted with the 2014 tsunami relief operations in a particular district recounted the following incident. He was with Amma when she received a phone call from the brahmacārī in charge of building houses for the victims of the tsunami. Amma asked him about the number of bricks and cement used to build each house. She also asked about the different colors of paint used. The Collector, who was listening attentively, later recounted during an event in Amṛtapuri, "Amma has so many responsibilities, and yet she notices things that we consider insignificant. Her management style is truly impressive!"

Amma points out that regular *sādhana* (spiritual practice) is as important as *sēvā* (selfless service). Once, I became lax in my sādhana, and justified my laziness on the grounds that I had a heavy workload at school. I barely did one *arcana* daily! During this time, I went for darśan. Usually, Amma whispers "my daughter," "my darling daughter" or "my little daughter" to me. This time, she whispered, "Are you my darling daughter?"

I was shaken. I got up and left without even looking at Amma; I did not dare to. Her voice resonated in my mind for days. I resolved from then on to become Amma's darling daughter again. I started doing my sādhana with care, focus and regularity. When I went for the next darśan, Amma whispered to me her usual reassuring, "My little daughter!"

Amma's love always brings us back to the path. She gives equal importance to *japa* (repeated chanting of a mantra),

---

14 An officer in the Indian Administrative Service who is responsible for the collection of land revenue and revenue administration, and who is the highest revenue judicial authority in the district.

meditation, scriptural study and sēvā. Doing sādhana regularly purifies the mind. Once it is purified, the ego is weakened and it becomes easier to surrender.

* * *

Amma came into my life in a unique way. The Dēvī idol in our family temple was leaning to one side. This was considered most inauspicious, and we believed that it was because of this that our family was facing many problems. The family elders advised us to perform a *punaḥ-pratiṣṭha* (re-installation), and one of our relatives suggested that we invite Amma to conduct the ceremony. Although we had heard of Amma, we had not met her yet. Someone asked Amma on our behalf, and she sent a brahmacārī from her āśram to perform the punaḥ-pratiṣṭha.

The date for the punaḥ-pratiṣṭha was scheduled during the harvest week. Our paddy field was quite far from our house. Since no workers were available there, my father used to take five or six workers from our place, and spend a week there. This time, however, some 40 workers became available unexpectedly, and my father was able to complete the harvesting in one day! Such a thing had never happened before. This incident gave my father faith in Amma.

Within two days, the preparations for the punaḥ-pratiṣṭha were completed. Father told us he had a surprise for us and asked us to go to the *pūjā* (prayer) room. When we went there, we saw a big photo of Amma in *Dēvī bhāva,* wearing a red blouse and a blue sari, a beautiful smile adorning her face. Her shining eyes, nose-ring, and jewelry were so captivating! My father explained it would be nice to have a photo of Amma since her disciple was coming to our house.

Br. Babu (now Br. Śrīdharāmṛta Caitanya) performed the punaḥ-pratiṣṭha ceremony in accordance with Amma's instructions. Before that, he performed a pūjā to Amma's photo. My father played his *uḍukku* (a small hand-held drum) to mark the occasion. Even though we had not met Amma yet, she graced our home and our hearts with her subtle presence. We started worshipping her, seeing her as Dēvī.

That year (1991), my sister and I had our first darśan during the Kodungalloor Brahmasthānam temple festival. From the moment we met Amma, we both wanted to stay with her. We hesitated to ask Amma about it, thinking that we might not be worthy. Once after darśan, I sat down crying. A little later, my sister went for darśan. Amma asked her, "'Didn't you just come for darśan?"

She replied, "'No, Amma, that was my twin sister."

Amma laughed loudly. Pointing to me, she told those around her, "See, one is crying there; the other one is here. They're twins. I have to look after both of them!"

When we heard this, we were thrilled, knowing that Amma had accepted us into her āśram.

As the only children of our parents, getting their permission to join the āśram was not easy. The moment we mentioned it, there was a chorus of wails and protests. Once, when we went to the āśram, my parents even came there to take us back. But, by Amma's grace, they changed their minds and willingly handed us over into Amma's holy hands.

Amma has always taken good care of us. Let me recount one more experience. I had been staying at the Pandalam school alone for some time when, one night, someone stole the battery of the school bus. I told Amma that I had since become gripped by fear, especially at night. I was hoping that she would allow the school to have a security guard at night. Amma said, "Daughter, keep a dog." The image of a white Pomeranian puppy came to mind. Amma continued, "Daughter, there's no need to buy an expensive breed; an ordinary dog will do. You must get a kennel. Since there are children in the school, the dog should not be let out during the day, only at night. It will also keep you company then."

But I was in no mood to rear a dog, especially some local mutt! I did not want the extra work of feeding a dog and making a kennel for it. With these thoughts, I traveled back to the school.

When I reached the school, I was astounded. There to welcome me was a family of dogs, which included the father, mother and children! Amma knew my mind, and instead of giving me just one dog, she gave me an entire family of canine security staff! They would leave in the mornings and arrive after sunset for duty. I had company all night and did not need to get a kennel for them.

Amma puts us through several trials to make us strong. She always tells us, "You are not lamps to be lit by others but the Self-effulgent sun." Or, "You're not bleating lambs but roaring lions." She tells us the story of the lion cub that grew up with a herd of sheep. The lion cub grew up believing it was also as meek as a lamb. One day, a lion came from the wild and told the cub that it was also a lion, just like him. But the cub could not accept this. The lion then showed the cub his reflection in a pond. The cub was amazed and became aware of its true potential.

Isn't this what Amma is also doing for us? Bit by bit, she is revealing our true potential to us. May we all be able to follow the path Amma is showing us and attain the Supreme.

18

Empire of Love

Br. Gauriśaṅkarāmṛta Caitanya

Karma refers to actions and includes both mundane activities such as eating and bathing as well as spiritual practices like *pūjā* (worship), *arcana* (chanting of divine names), *japa* (repetition of a mantra) and the study of scriptures. When actions are done worshipfully with a view to attaining God, karma becomes *karma yōga*. For spiritual seekers, all actions ought to be aimed at *citta śuddhi*, or purifying the mind and intellect. If we can perform all actions with such one-pointedness, we can attain *Brahma-jñāna*, knowledge of the Supreme.

Those who are completely absorbed in God consciousness understand the following:

> *brahmārpaṇam brahma havir brahmāgnau brahmaṇā hutam*
> *brahmaiva tena gantavyam brahma karma samādhinā*
> Brahman is the ritual sacrifice. Brahman is the oblation (sacred offering), which is offered by Brahman to the fire of Brahman. One who sees Brahman in everything attains Brahman. (*Bhagavad Gītā*, 4.24)

This is the sacred verse I have chanted the most since joining the āśram. We chant it before meals, and is hence also known as the *bhōjana* (food) *mantra*. However, it is not meant only to be chanted before eating; we must also strive to assimilate the principle behind this verse, which is a pointer towards the ultimate truth.

The food we eat orally is offered to the digestive fire. But we also consume through other sense organs; all that we see, hear and feel is food for them. That is why the sages said:

> *bhadram karṇēbhiḥ śṛṇuyāma dēvaḥ*
> *bhadram paśyēmakṣabhir-yajatrāḥ...*
> O gods, may we hear auspicious words with the ears; may we see auspicious things with the eyes... (*Ṛgvēda*, 1:89.8)

Just as eating stale food can cause food poisoning, seeing or hearing unwanted things can pollute the mind. Hence, the sages prayed to perceive only the auspicious. Today, the mass media bombards us with all kinds of audio-visuals. Can we enjoy them without becoming affected by them? Completely impossible! Amma says it is very difficult not to salivate when the tongue comes into contact with sugar. The only way to protect the mind is to stay away physically and mentally from stimuli that can cause negative impressions.

I recall a story that Amma narrates. Two disciples in an āśram were quarreling with each other. When their master came to know about it, he summoned them both and asked them what happened. One disciple said, “Master, he called me a donkey!”

The other disciple retorted, “That’s because he called me a monkey first!”

Hearing this, the master said, “For the last 10 years, I’ve been teaching you that you are Brahman, but you never paid attention to that. Yet, when someone called you a donkey or monkey, you reacted instantly!"

Most of us identify with our body and mind. Only if we follow the Guru's instructions and focus on *sādhana* (spiritual practice) and *sēvā* (selfless service) to attain inner purity can we realize that our true self is Brahman. Merely saying "I am Brahman" will not take us anywhere. We should be able to experience that state. Sages experienced this truth only after years of penance. Scriptural dicta are nothing but the distillations of the sublime experiences of sages.

Once, a group of brahmacārīs decided not to go for their sēvā, saying that knowledge (*jñāna*) is greater than action (*karma*), and hence, the path of contemplation was better. They said, "We are Brahman. Amma also says the same thing. Therefore, there is no need for sēvā."

When Amma heard about this, she called all the brahmacārīs to her room. All of us somehow managed to squeeze into her room. Amma said, "You eat. That is also karma. Will you sit still if you don't get food and continue proclaiming that you are Brahman? Do you see pure consciousness when you see a beautiful woman?"

Most of us dwell in duality. Spiritual masters abide in a state of non-duality. We should strive to gain the latter experience. The words '*Tat tvam asi*'—'You are That'—are emblazoned in front of the Sabarimala temple, and yet how many pilgrims truly realize this great saying? Amma starts all her talks by saying, "Amma bows down to everyone, who are embodiments of pure love and the supreme self." When she ends, she says, "Amma offers these words to the Supreme." Amma sees everyone and everything as an embodiment of the Supreme. The way Amma gave darśan to Dattan, the leper, and healed him would be unimaginable to anyone else. Only someone who is one with God can see the Divine in everyone. Have we ever wondered why we don't experience the Truth when Amma addresses us all as embodiments of the Supreme? It is because our mind and intellect believe otherwise.

The ego will dissolve only when we surrender completely. In that state, if the Guru utters "Tat tvam asi," there will not be an 'I' that thinks differently. The Guru's words will go straight to the heart of the disciple, who will then realize the Truth: *'Aham Brahmāsmi'*—'I am the Supreme.'

One night, I was engaged in my sēvā of pumping water into the tank. To overcome my sleepiness, I started tidying up the electrical room and played the bhajan *'Ānanda Vīthiyil.'* Only Amma's voice can be heard in that bhajan. Just then, Amma returned from the beach after meditation, and hearing the bhajan, came into the electrical room. She looked inside and saw that I was working. As I was completely absorbed in my work, I was not aware that Amma was standing at the door. She stood there for some time before leaving. I only found out about Amma's visit later, when another brahmacārī told me about it. Either directly or indirectly, Amma knows our every action. When we work for her, work becomes worship.

Unlike other religions, Sanātana Dharma[15] proclaims that anyone can become divine. Amma is living proof of this proclamation. If the disciple is ready, he or she can realize the Self in a trice.

---

15 'Eternal Religion' or 'Eternal Way of Life,' the original or traditional name of Hinduism.

The story of King Janaka is a wonderful case in point. Once while traveling, he saw Sage Aṣṭāvakra, so named because his body was twisted in eight places. Though a young teenager, the sage was radiant with the light of Self-realization. Perceiving his divinity, the king prostrated in front of Aṣṭāvakra and begged for ultimate knowledge. Aṣṭāvakra asked Janaka to meet him alone in the forest. This indicates that we are alone in the quest for spiritual knowledge. Only the Guru can help us.

After finding Aṣṭāvakra in the forest, King Janaka repeated his request. Aṣṭāvakra replied, "I need a *Guru dakṣiṇa.*"[16]

Janaka replied, "My kingdom and all its wealth are yours. Please accept them and bestow on me eternal wisdom."

Aṣṭāvakra said, "I need something more precious than your kingdom and all its wealth."

Confused, Janaka asked, "O Guru, what is that?"

Aṣṭāvakra smilingly replied, "Your mind."

Janaka surrendered his mind and was liberated instantly. When we have complete surrender, a fraction of a second is enough for the flow of the Guru's grace to uplift us. To attain this attitude of surrender, the mind must be pure. It is to help us acquire mental purity that Amma tells us to do sēvā. Only when we have complete surrender can Amma elevate us to the state of Brahman.

I was born into a family that followed another religion. How did I reach Amma? Was there a *saṅkalpa* (divine resolve) that enabled me to reach this divine abode? How did I become capable of doing things I have never done before in my life? I have only

---

16 Honorarium given to the Guru as a token of the disciple's gratitude and appreciation.

one answer: Amma. She is that pure Brahman we worship and seek.

My life was a struggle before I joined the āśram. Everyone in my family was a daily wage earner. However, our earnings were so meager that we lived in abject poverty. On many occasions, I went to the forest and plucked fruits to appease my hunger. Because we were so poor, I did not get a proper education either.

I heard about Amma and came to see her. I asked her whether I could stay in the āśram. Amma smiled but did not say anything. I started visiting the āśram frequently. Seeing this, members from my place of worship started to abuse me verbally and physically. I told Amma everything and she asked me, "Son, are you afraid?"

I replied, "If Amma is with me, I'm not afraid of anyone."

Amma replied, "Go back home for now. Amma will take care of everything. The next time you come, tell them that you are going somewhere else. Don't bring a busload of people here, as you usually do!"

After returning home, I found out that some people from the place of worship had filed a case against me. I then understood why Amma had sent me back. I continued visiting the āśram frequently for the next two years, after which, Amma gave me permission to stay here.

When a tsunami struck the āśram in 2004, Amma supervised the rescue operations. After evacuating everyone, the swāmīs requested Amma to take shelter at the university campus across the backwaters. Amma said, "How can I leave when our cows and elephants are here? I'm not going anywhere!"

Hearing this, I asked Amma, "Can the cows be accommodated in the Kālī temple? I can take the elephants to the other side of the backwaters."

Amma asked, "How will you take the elephants across? What if the water level rises again?"

I replied, "I'll walk them there. With Amma's grace, the water will not rise."

"How long will it take to bring them to the other side?"

"It will take an hour to cross the bridge at Panikkar Kadavu."

Amma said, "Alright. After you come back, Amma will go to the university."

It was my strong faith in Amma that enabled me to make these suggestions. By her grace, I could take the elephants across the bridge to the Amrita Vidyalayam (school) in Puthiyakavu and come back. Amma inquired if I had arranged food and accommodation for the mahouts and the elephants, Rām and Lakṣmī. It was only after I assured her that everything had been arranged for them that Amma was ready to take the boat to the university. By then, it was 7 p.m.

Amma's empire of love includes all sentient and insentient beings. Just like us, animals also jostle for a place near her. Amma recounted an incident involving two of the āśram dogs, Tumban and Bhakti. Once, when Bhakti was lying next to Amma, Tumban nosed Bhakti away so that he could lie next to Amma.

For Amma, there is no difference between human or animal. She sees the Self in all beings. Swāmī Pūrṇāmṛtānanda has narrated how Amma once fed a rabid dog with her hand and then ate food from the same plate without washing her hand. This incident is a powerful demonstration of the fearlessness that arises from the vision of the oneness of all beings and of the love that arises from the experience of oneness. This is the practical benefit of the experience of Brahman: it makes us compassionate towards all beings.

Our goal is to realize Amma; realizing Amma is realizing oneself. This is the ultimate knowledge. When Lord Kṛṣṇa was about to unveil his universal form to Arjuna, he first had to bestow divine sight upon the disciple so that Arjuna could behold that form. Similarly, Amma alone can enable us to realize her true nature. Let us pray for Amma's blessings.

19

Serving Others, Serving God.

Bri. Satyapriyāmṛta Caitanyā

In the *Bhagavad Gītā*, Lord Kṛṣṇa begins by singing the glories of Self-knowledge to Arjuna. Shortly, he tells Arjuna to take up arms and fight. Hearing this, the latter becomes confused. Was he to gain knowledge of the Self or to act? Seeking to clarify his doubts, he asks the Lord which of the two paths was better. In response, Lord Kṛṣṇa elucidates two paths to becoming a spiritual adept: *karma yōga* (path of action) and *jñāna yōga* (path of knowledge):

> *lōkē'smin dvividhā niṣṭhā purā prōktā mayānagha*
> *jñānayōgēna sāṅkhyānām karmayōgēna yōginām*
> O sinless one, as previously explained, there is a two-fold path in this world: the path of knowledge for the Sāṅkhyas (those inclined towards contemplation) and the path of action for the Yōgīs (those inclined towards action). (3.3)

Arjuna's doubt is like that of a patient who asks, "Which is better, medicine or surgery?" The answer depends on the nature of the patient's illness and the degree of its severity. Similarly, the Guru recommends either the path of jñāna or that of karma based on the seeker's maturity.

Amma explains this in a simple way. She says that people have different tastes. Some enjoy eating ripe jackfruit; some prefer it boiled and others like it fried. Though tastes may vary, the goal is the same: to appease hunger. Similarly, the path to God may differ but the goal is Self-realization. What is important is that we start from where we are and proceed towards God from there. Lord Kṛṣṇa says as much:

> *yataḥ pravṛttir bhūtānām yēna sarvam idam tatam*
> *sva karmaṇā tam abhyarcya siddhim vindati mānavaḥ*
> Doing one's duties is worship of the Creator, from whom all beings have evolved and who pervades everything. Doing such work, one easily attains perfection. (18.46)

Service to others is service to God. He has given us the body, mind, intelligence and/or wealth with which to serve others. We have nothing to call our own. Therefore, the only way in which we can repay God is by serving others.

In the *Bhagavad Gītā*, Lord Kṛṣṇa says all *karma* (actions) must evolve into karma yōga. To enable this, we must act selflessly and with an attitude of complete surrender to the Lord. Some say that karma is binding, but the truth is that actions can neither bind nor free anyone. It is the intention behind the action that results in bondage or freedom.

The following story, which Amma narrates, explains this. Seeing a few sculptors at work, a passer-by asked one of them, "Sir, what are you doing?"

Without even lifting his head to look at the questioner, the sculptor muttered, "Can't you see what I'm doing?"

The passer-by moved on and repeated his question to the next sculptor, who put his tools down, looked up at the man, sighed deeply and said, "I'm struggling to make ends meet!"

The passer-by walked to another sculptor, who was joyfully humming a tune while working. The man asked him the same thing. Hearing the question, the sculptor smiled pleasantly and said, "I'm creating a statue!"

Though all three were doing the same work, their attitudes were different. For the first worker, work was drudgery, and for the second, it was a means of livelihood. The third worker alone derived joy from work. Like the third sculptor, we must learn how to make all work a blissful experience.

Many years ago, one of my *sēvās* (service duties) was to collect and deliver lunch to the elderly women in the āśram's hospital. If there were any leftovers, the person bringing the food was expected to finish it and not waste it. This meant that I often had to eat leftover lunch for dinner while everyone else was having fresh *kañññi* (rice gruel). After some time, I got fed up with this situation.

Around this time, it was announced that we had to go to Ernakulam for *Amritavarsham50*, Amma's 50th birthday celebrations. I was delighted, thinking that I would be relieved from my food delivery sēvā for at least a few days. During *Amritavarsham50*, my sēvā was at the juice stall. I assumed that I would be able to do my sēvā and enjoy all the cultural programs as well.

When I went to the juice stall on the first day, I saw that many volunteers had come to help. However, to get food during mealtimes, they would have to walk quite a distance through thick crowds and wait in long queues. The juice stall supervisor suggested that I bring food for the volunteers from the āśram residents' food counter so that the volunteers could continue their sēvā during meal times. I ended up carrying all their meals from the food counter to the juice stall!

That was when I understood the meaning of the Malayāḷam proverb, '*Maḍiyan mala cumakkum*' — 'The lazy one will be made to carry the mountain.' Forget watching all the cultural programs, I could not even step into the stadium (program venue) during the celebrations!

When I returned to the āśram, my attitude towards my food delivery sēvā changed completely. I began to see work as a form of worship and was able to do it happily. What brought about this change in my attitude was observing Amma at work. Whatever she does — whether giving darśan, cleaning up public spaces, sewing masks, planting vegetables on her terrace or chopping vegetables — is almost always for someone else.

After *Amritavarsham50* ended, I returned on September 28th to the āśram along with some other brahmacāriṇīs, as I had to resume my hospital sēvā. None of us thought that Amma would come out on the 29th, but she came to the Kālī temple for meditation and to give darśan to her international children, knowing that they would leave in a day or two, even though she had been giving darśan continuously for hours on end the previous days. Selflessness is Amma's hallmark. Her only goal is to help others and make them happy.

Many of Amma's children have been inspired by Amma's example of serving others selflessly. I recall the selfless actions of an āśram resident, C.G. Ramachandran (whom we call C.G.R. Acchan). Once, at the end of a North Indian Tour, I was returning to Mumbai from the Howrah Railway Station in Kolkata. Some āśram residents were returning to Amṛtapuri. Though we left the Kolkata āśram early, heavy traffic delayed our arrival at the station. My train was far away from the trains the other āśram residents were boarding; it would take about half an hour to walk to where my train was. However, as my train was scheduled to leave first, C.G.R. Acchan escorted me to my train, even though this meant that he would have to walk a long way to his platform and even though we had never been acquainted before. Owing to the rush of commuters, we could not move quickly. Seeing that my train was about to depart, Acchan carried my heavy luggage on his head and started running towards it. The moment I boarded the train, it started moving. I was unable to thank C.G.R. Acchan for his selfless gesture.

Amma says that we are all one. It is to gain this sublime understanding that we do *sādhana* (spiritual practices). Amma says that when we offer flowers to God during worship, we are the first ones to enjoy the beauty and fragrance of the flowers. Similarly, when we serve others, we are the ones who benefit. God does not need anything from us. It is we who need the knowledge that we are all spiritually one. In the *Bhagavad Gītā*, Lord Kṛṣṇa says, "*Tatsvayam yōgasamsiddhaḥ kālēnātmani vindati*"—"One who has perfected oneself through yōga discovers this knowledge in due course of time" (4.38).

To gain this knowledge, the scriptures suggest the four-fold spiritual practices known as *sādhana catuṣṭaya*:

1. *vivēka*: discriminating between the ephemeral and the eternal;
2. *vairāgya*: dispassion towards worldly pleasures;
3. *ṣaṭ-samapatti*: gaining the six-fold spiritual wealth that includes *śama* (control over the senses), *dama* (control

over the mind), *uparati* (withdrawal of mind from sensory pleasures), *titikṣā* (forbearance), *śraddhā* (faith in the Guru, God and the scriptures) and *samādhāna* (steadfast concentration); and

4. *mumukṣutva* – an intense desire for spiritual liberation.

Those who have purified their mind through selfless service and contemplation alone are fit to receive the highest wisdom. Amma says that if we pour milk into a dirty vessel, the milk will get spoiled. We need to clean the vessel first. Similarly, only when the mind becomes purified do we become worthy of spiritual wisdom.

One of the mantras in the *Lalitā Sahasranāma* (1,000 names of the Divine Mother) is '*Ōm paśu pāśa vimōcinyai namaḥ*' — 'Salutations to the Divine Mother, who releases the ignorant from bondage' (354). One who lives without self-control and according to the whims and fancies of his mind is no better than an animal (*paśu*) that has been tied to the pole of life with the rope (*pāśa*) of karma. When the sword of knowledge severs this rope, the *jīva* (individual soul) is no more a paśu but becomes *Paśupati* (one who is victorious over his animalistic tendencies), Lord Śiva himself. This is clearly stated in the *Bhagavad Gītā*: '*aśvattham-ēnam suvirūḍha-mūlam asaṅga-śastrēṇa dṛḍhēna chittvā*' — 'this deep-rooted tree of ignorance must be uprooted by the sword of discrimination' (15.3).

To awaken this faculty of discernment and gain Self-knowledge, the *Bhagavad Gītā* says that we must approach a *mahātmā*, a knower of the truth:

tad-viddhi praṇipātēna paripraśnēna sēvayā
upadēkṣyanti tē jñānam jñāninas-tattva-darśinaḥ

> By humbly submitting to the wise, by asking them questions, and by serving them, they, who have realized the Truth, will impart wisdom to you. (4.34)

Once, a king named Sadhaka Varma desired to gain this wisdom. He had heard of how King Parīkṣit had attained Self-knowledge by attending a seven-day recital of the *Bhāgavata Purāṇa* by Sage Śuka. King Varma invited a renowned scholar of the *Bhāgavata Purāṇa* for a recital at his court. But even after listening to the glories of the Lord, the king did not realize the Self. When he asked why, the scholar became tongue-tied. He returned home and pondered the king's question. Seeing him deep in thought, his daughter asked him why he was worried. The scholar related to her the king's question. The daughter, who was intelligent, told her father that she would solve his problem.

The next day, she went to the palace and announced that she had come in lieu of her father to clarify the king's doubt. But before that, she wanted one condition to be fulfilled: the king must agree to being tied to a pillar for some time. The king agreed. Then the girl requested that she be tied to another pillar. A little later, she told the king, "I'm bound to this pillar by these ropes. I cannot untie the ropes myself. Could you please help me?"

The king replied, "Child, how can I possibly do so when I am bound myself?"

The girl then said, "O King, this is the answer to the question you asked yesterday. Sage Śuka was a liberated soul and was hence able to lead King Parīkṣit towards Self-realization. But my scholar-father is still bound to the world. How can he guide you to the highest goal in life?" Hearing this, the king's doubt was completely removed.

It is said in the *Śrīmad Bhāgavatam*, "*Ātmārāmāśca munayō nirgranthāḥ*" — "Those who revel in the Self and the sages are free from all bonds" (1.7.10). How can the blind lead the blind? Only a lighted lamp can light other lamps. Similarly, only a Self-realized soul can lead humanity to Self-realization.

Even if we study the *Upaniṣads*, the *ṣaḍ-darśanas* (six systems of Hindu philosophy) and the *Mahābhārata*, we need the guidance of a Guru like Amma to grasp the principles of these texts. If this guidance is missing, our scholarship will not be of much help to us or to others.

Amma says that what makes our life blessed are meditative action and compassion. Acting without awareness or knowledge is like trying to fill a tank with water only to discover later that all the water we poured in has drained away because of a hole in the tank. Jñāna and karma are interdependent. The aim of both karma yōga and jñāna yōga is to attain the highest wisdom. We can walk either path. If we stick to one path and strive continuously, we can attain the knowledge that liberates. A yōgī is one who sees that, in essence, both karma yōga and jñāna yōga are the same.

* * *

I heard about Amma when Bri. Kamalam-*cēcci*[17] told my mother about her. I first visited Amṛtapuri in 1992. I was in the 8th grade. As I stood in front of the āśram, it seemed very familiar. "I shall live and die here," was the thought that passed through

17 *'Older sister' in Malayāḷam.*

my mind. When I received Amma's darśan, I found myself drawn to her divine love. I later read Amma's message in *Matruvani*, in which it was said that we do not need to drink the whole ocean to know its taste; a sip is enough. Likewise, a few experiences are enough to help us understand the nature of the world. These words touched me, and I began to contemplate Amma's words more often.

In 1998, I joined the Amrita Pharmacy college at the Kalloor āśram for my higher studies. I wanted to join the āśram after that. It was during this time that I heard Swāmī Pūrṇāmṛtānanda explain the meaning of the verse quoted earlier: *'tad-viddhi praṇipātēna...'* He explained that when we want to ask the Guru something, we need to frame our question properly. I began thinking of how best to ask Amma.

When I went for darśan, I asked, "Amma, will you accept me as your disciple?" She agreed at once. I went back to Kalloor, finished my studies, and joined the āśram a few months later.

Since childhood, I have had a strong desire to take care of the dying. I felt that one could live properly only when one has understood death. Soon after joining the āśram, I was asked to serve at Amma's Cancer Hospice in Badlapur in Maharashtra, India. There, I met a woman who had been working at the hospice for many years. I asked her, "Knowing that death is inevitable for these patients, many people shy away from this place. Don't you feel any fear working here?"

She said, "Why should I fear? This is my Guru's abode. If I work here, I will receive her grace."

Once, an astrologer examining my horoscope asked me if I had any problems with my leg. I said that I did not. Hearing this, he said that it was by divine grace alone that I could walk. He added that according to my chart, I should have been bedridden with a terminal illness. I realized that by my serving the patients in the hospice, Amma had altered the course of my destiny.

The *Bhagavad Gītā* does not mention idol worship but extols service to humankind. Lord Kṛṣṇa declares that those who are compassionate to all beings (‘*dayā bhūtēṣu*’) are of a divine nature (16.2), and that those who are ever engaged in serving others (‘*sarva-bhūta hitē ratāḥ*’) become one with God (12.4).

May Amma bless us all with the insight to see our sēvā as service to God.

20
Equal Vision

Br. Swātmā Caitanya

Mahātmās (spiritually illumined being) face adverse situations with perfect equanimity. Their calm behavior can seem strange to ordinary people. The story of Jaḍa Bharata is a great example. He was born into a traditional Brahmin family but never showed any attachment towards his parents or to traditions. He was always silent and would not do anything unless asked, and then he would help without any hesitation. People did not know what to make of him and called him *jaḍa*, inert. But actually, he was an *avadhūta*—an enlightened being whose behavior is often eccentric and at odds with social norms. But without understanding his elevated state, people would take advantage of him and make him work for them.

The king of Sauvīra was searching for a palanquin bearer. He already had three bearers and needed a fourth. Royal servants saw Jaḍa Bharata and thought he would make a good, strong candidate. They took him to the king. The king was traveling to Sage Kapila's āśram near River Ikṣumatī. The other three bearers were walking at the same speed. Jaḍa Bharata was moving slowly to avoid stepping on insects and other creatures; he was observing *ahimsā* (non-violence). As a result, the movement of the palanquin became uneven and lurching. Annoyed, the king looked out to find out what was happening. When he saw how Jaḍa Bharata was moving, he stepped out of the palanquin, yelled at him and slapped him, but Jaḍa Bharata did not react. The king realized that there was something unusual about him. He asked, "I shouted at you and slapped you. But you didn't react. Why not?"

For the first time in his life, Jaḍa Bharata opened his mouth and spoke: "O King, you see only this or that body. But in reality, we are not the body, which you think is ours. Similarly, when we say 'I,' we are not referring to the body. We are in reality the Self, which is beyond the body. The Self has neither health nor disease. It is not even bearing your palanquin."

Hearing these words of spiritual wisdom, the king recognized Jaḍa Bharata's divinity and prostrated before him.

The Self is not the doer or enjoyer. We impose those notions on the Self. One who fully realizes this truth is an *ātma-jñānī* or Knower of the Self. Such a person sees the Self in himself and in others, even amidst adverse situations. He sees everything with perfect equanimity and with equal vision.

In the *Bhagavad Gītā*, Lord Kṛṣṇa says:

> *vidyā-vinaya-sampannē brāhmaṇē gavi hastini*
> *śuni caiva śwapākē ca paṇḍitāḥ sama-darśinaḥ*
>
> The wise, who are learned and humble, regard a Brahmin, a cow, an elephant, a dog and even a dog-eater with an equal eye. (5.18)

Here, the word '*paṇḍita*' does not indicate a scholar. '*Paṇḍa*' is an intellect that is fixed on the Self. Hence, one whose intellect is fixed on the Self is known as a paṇḍita.

In ancient times, a Brahmin was respected by everyone whereas a dog-eater was a social outcaste. However, an ātma-jñani regards everyone equally, and does not distinguish between the respected or the despised. He sees the same self in all beings in the universe. The 6th chapter of the *Bhagavad Gītā* explains this state of equanimity:

> *sarva-bhūta-stham ātmānaṁ sarva-bhūtāni cātmani*
> *īkṣatē yōga-yuktātmā sarvatra sama-darśanaḥ*
> The true yōgī, who has united his consciousness with God, regards everyone equally and hence sees all living beings in God and God in all living beings. (6.29)

One whose consciousness is fixed on the Self perceives it shining behind the apparent variety in creation. Such a person sees the one Self in the entire universe. In wooden chairs and tables, the common denominator amidst the differences in form and function is wood. Amma often says that the Creator and creation are the same. The unmanifest *nirguṇa* (essence without attributes) is present in the manifest form, which has attributes (*saguṇa*). Similarly, attributes are latent in the unmanifest. A jñānī knows this and has the conviction that the universe is nothing but the manifest form of the unmanifest Brahman (the Supreme). There are waves and ripples in the ocean; its essence, though, is water. Likewise, a jñanī sees Brahman as the essence of the entire universe.

Equanimity comes naturally to Self-realized masters, whereas we must put in effort to cultivate it. Equal vision means seeing the Self in all beings always. It means going beyond notions of superiority and inferiority and accepting the totality of all life. For most of us, notions of superiority and inferiority are deep rooted.

Two incidents from the life of Śrī Rāmakṛṣṇa illustrate how he used different methods to eradicate the subtle notions of superiority and inferiority from his mind. As a Brahmin, he was expected to adhere to rules of purity. For instance, he was not allowed to enter an outcaste's house. But he would go to such a house and clean it with his long hair! Śrī Rāmakṛṣṇa would also go to the banks of the Ganges. Holding gold in one hand and sand in the other, he would throw both away in the river. What would we have done in his place? We would have thrown the sand in the river and pocketed the gold. We need not imitate the actions of Śrī Rāmakṛṣṇa. We need money to buy necessities, but we must understand that it cannot give us peace. What we need to discard is greed.

When we read Amma's biography, we can see that she was born Self-realized. Like Śrī Rāmakṛṣṇa, she also performed sādhana but did it to set an example to the world. In her early years, Amma would sleep and eat outside, immersed in meditation most of the time. Mother Nature would protect and provide for her. One day, Amma came out of meditation feeling hungry. A cow came running and showed her udder to Amma, inviting her to drink. This cow became a regular provider for Amma, patiently waiting for her to come out of meditation to give her milk. There were many such instances. Amma sees nothing as different from her. She is one with all of creation.

It is our ego, with its likes and dislikes, that keeps us away from this kind of God-consciousness. The ego is like a pot immersed in a vast ocean. The water in the pot is not different from the water outside. Likewise, in the vastness of consciousness, we have created a separate ego that keeps us in a state of misery. The *Chāndōgya Upaniṣad* says,

> *sarvam khalvidam brahma tajjalāniti śānta upāsīta atha khalu kratumayaḥ puruṣaḥ*
>
> All this undoubtedly is Brahman. Everything comes from, is sustained by, and goes back to Brahman. Hence, one should meditate serenely on Brahman. Man is a creation of his own thoughts and desires. (3.14.1)

The scriptures say that Brahman pervades everything, including water, earth, air and space. This does not mean that the perishable elements are God but that He is the imperishable essence in everything. Worshipping God through an idol will benefit us, but we should progress from there. Only when we see God in everyone and everything will we get the ultimate benefit of idol worship. When we start to perceive all objects as a manifestation of the Divine, and perform all our actions as worship of God, we will gradually be able to go beyond our limited ego and experience true peace of mind.

There is only one way to gain peace of mind—we must overcome the hindrances in our minds. Our discriminating intellect is always seeing differences, and this creates aversion. Hatred towards someone might not harm that person but it will harm us. It will destroy our peace of mind. We must overcome aversion if we wish to progress in meditation. We will make progress only when we start to see God in everyone and everything.

Let us look at how Amma trains us. She tells us to do both sādhana and *sēvā* (selfless service). These practices slowly reduce the power of our likes and dislikes. To help us overcome our ego, she gives us work that we dislike, but she also showers her love on us, thereby helping us gain the peace and inner strength to do more sēvā.

I went through this kind of training when I first joined the āśram. My first sēvā was at the bookstall, where I served for many years. Maybe because of that, I developed a liking for this sēvā. Then one day, Amma told me, "There are enough people in the bookstall. From today onwards, you should go to the College and serve food in the students' dining hall three times a day." Even though I obeyed Amma, I did not like this new sēvā at all. I disliked the physical work involved. Not only that, no matter how careful I was, the curry would always stain my clothing. Of course, I knew these were not reasons for leaving this sēvā, but I went to Amma after some time to explain that fewer people were working in the bookstall and told her that I would like to return to my previous sēvā. Amma lovingly asked me to continue my sēvā at the students' dining hall and sent someone else instead to the bookstall. Having no other choice, I accepted the dining hall sēvā with all my heart. With my new attitude of acceptance, the work that had seemed so hard in the beginning became joyful. I started feeling more peace and inner freedom than I had ever experienced before. This experience taught me that if we accept God's will, we will reap the benefits of surrendering. Our negative tendencies are so deeply rooted that we feel that they are part of us. We cannot imagine that we would ever be able to overcome them and move forward. But mahātmās tell us that we can gradually go beyond the mind and its tendencies and gain real wisdom.

In *Tattvōpadēśa*, Śrī Śaṅkara declares, *"Bhāvādwaitam sadā kuryāt kriyādwaitam na karhicit"* — "We must constantly cultivate the attitude of non-duality but be discerning in our actions" (87). For example, even though God pervades everything, including water, we will not drink water from a toilet bowl. Although divine consciousness is all-pervading, we must acknowledge the rules of the game of life and play accordingly.

Returning to the verse from the *Bhagavad Gītā* quoted earlier, Lord Kṛṣṇa is encouraging us to cultivate the desire for Self-knowledge and to gain equal vision. The first two qualities we need to attain Self-knowledge are *vivēka* (discernment) and *vairāgya* (dispassion). The next six qualities are *śama* (control over the mind), *dama* (control over the senses), *uparati* (withdrawal), *titikṣā* (forbearance), *śraddhā* (faith), *samādhāna* (fixing the mind on God) and *mumukṣutva* (desire for spiritual liberation). When we have cultivated these qualities, we can enjoy both material and spiritual growth.

Almost all religions give importance to *mantra japa* or the repetition of sacred words. Swāmī Rāma Tīrtha says that if our mind is still inclined to external objects in spite of doing mantra japa, it indicates that we are not doing mantra japa properly. If we properly chant the mantra that the Guru gives us, our mind will turn inwards and we will experience inner peace.

Some people think that when we remove the ego, the Self will manifest automatically, but actually, it is the opposite: When we realize the Self, the ego or our limited individuality will disappear automatically, just as darkness disappears when light dawns. Darkness is not something that can be moved from one place to another. We have mistaken the Self for the body, mind and intellect. When we identify ourselves with the body, mind, and intellect, we become identified with the ego. But when we realize that we are the light that is manifesting as the body, mind and intellect, then Self-knowledge will dawn in us. Amma gives an example of moving inside a dark and cluttered room. We will bump into furniture and hurt ourselves. But as soon as we turn on the light, none of the objects will hinder our movement. We will be able to walk freely. In the same way, once the light of Self-knowledge dawns within us, we will easily be able to navigate the obstacles in life.

We can become qualified for Self-knowledge only with the guidance of a Guru. We must approach the Guru with utmost devotion. A verse in the *Muṇḍakōpaniṣad* explains this approach:

> *parīkṣya lōkān karmacitān brāhmaṇō nirvēdamāyān*
> *nāstyakṛtaḥ kṛtēna*
> *tadvijñānārtham sa gurumēvābhigacchēt samitpāṇiḥ*
> *śrōtriyam brahmaniṣṭham*
>
> May the earnest seeker, having examined the world produced by action, understand that no action can ever give rise to anything eternal, and thus become dispassionate. To attain knowledge of the eternal, let him approach a Guru, who is well-versed in the scriptures and established in the Supreme, with an attitude of service or humility. (12)

We may not be earnest seekers. Nevertheless, Amma still has the power to uplift us. She does not assess the worthiness of her children. She just gathers us all and leads us towards the goal. In reality, the Guru is our own true self. Whether we sing paeans in praise of her or bring her down to our level, the Guru always abides in the Self. Amma's glory lies in the fact that she has transcended the body, mind, and intellect.

From the first time I met Amma, I was firmly convinced that she was complete and above the dualities of joy and sorrow. But after living in the āśram for some time, a doubt arose in my mind. Amma seemed to be experiencing joy and sorrow, just like us. I wondered if it was possible to face so much adversity without getting affected. During my next room darśan, I asked her, "Amma, you seem to be experiencing joys and sorrows. How are you able to stay above all these experiences, even in their midst?"

Amma's answer was spontaneous and beautiful, "Son, for Amma, worldly experiences are trivial." She explained with an example. "Once the sun rises, what is the relevance of moonlight? Then it makes no difference at all whether the moon exists or not." Similarly, when the sun that is Amma dawns in our heart, all worldly experiences will fade into insignificance.

It is not that worldly experiences disappear for one who has attained Self-realization but they have no relevance for a mahātmā. Once we experience the Self, we will transcend the experiences of joy and sorrow, and be able to accept everything with an equal vision. May we all attain this goal.

21

The Mother Avatār

Bri. Sarvāmrita Caitanyā

Bhārat (India) is the spiritual light of the world. The Mother of the Universe incarnated here as Bhavatāriṇī, the form of Goddess Kālī who takes us across the ocean of transmigration. She has both a physical form and a subtle form. Amma incarnated for each and every one of her children. She is *avyāja karuṇā mūrtī,* the embodiment of pure compassion. No matter where we may be in the world, Amma resides in our hearts.

Amma could have selected any place for her birth, but she chose to be born into difficult circumstances. That is her greatness. The adversities of her life can be compared to Śrī Kṛṣṇa's. He was born in a prison. There was nothing favorable about his situation, but the Lord had only one aim: to guide people to God-realization. Amma was born in a remote village. The people here knew only about temple worship. They knew nothing about Gurus or āśrams. But Amma overcame all these obstacles and transformed this place into a global spiritual center.

Unfavorable circumstances are never obstacles for avatārs (divine incarnations). They can overcome any situation to fulfill their mission. In doing so, they may not enjoy the support or approval of society. Part of Amma's mission is to uplift women in society. She taught us (brahmacāriṇīs) *hōmas* (religious fire ceremonies) and sent us to Brahmasthānam temples to perform pūjās that were traditionally performed only by men.

Ultimately, all avatārs are concerned only with one thing: *dharma* (righteousness), which is eternal. In Chapter 4 of the *Bhagavad Gītā*, Kṛṣṇa tells Arjuna that the knowledge he is imparting is eternal, and that, at the beginning of creation, he taught it to the sun god, Vivaswān, who in turn taught it to Manu, the progenitor of mankind. Manu taught it to his son Ikṣvāku and the knowledge was passed through the ages. But in the course of time, this knowledge was lost. When Arjuna heard this, he wondered how Kṛṣṇa could have taught the sun god so long ago. The Lord explained, "You and I have passed through several births. You do not remember them, but I know all of them. I am without birth. I am the God of all creation, and my nature is imperishable. I manifest in the world by virtue of my divine power." (*Bhagavad Gītā*, 4.5 - 6)

Kṛṣṇa further adds:

> *yadā yadā hi dharmasya glānir bhavati bhārata*
> *abhyutthānam adharmasya tadātmānam sṛjāmyaham*
> *paritrāṇāya sādhūnām vināśāya ca duṣkṛtām*
> *dharma-samsthāpanārthāya sambhavāmi yugē yugē*
>
> O Arjuna, whenever righteousness wanes and unrighteousness flourishes, I manifest myself on earth. I appear on earth, age after age, to protect the righteous, to annihilate the wicked, and to reestablish the principles of dharma. (4.7 – 8)

This was Śrī Kṛṣṇa's message of hope to the world: that God incarnates in every age to restore dharma, to protect the noble, and to remove evil. The Lord began his mission from the time he was born. One of his first expressions of this was the killing of Pūtanā. Pūtanā means *'pūtān api ākarṣate'*—'one who attracts even good people.' When she came to Vṛndāvan, the villagers failed to recognize her for the demoness she truly was. She came in the guise of a wet nurse, and all the babies she suckled died. But baby Kṛṣṇa knew that she had come to kill him. He could have strangled her easily, but by drinking her milk, he bestowed spiritual liberation on her.

Dharma is defined thus: *'dhārayati iti dharmaḥ'*—'that which sustains the universal balance or order.' Some of the fundamental principles of dharma are truth, non-violence, renunciation, and sense control. A society that stops adhering to these principles starts to decline. Of the four *puruṣārthas* (human pursuits), the most important is dharma. A man who tries to gain wealth unrighteously eventually paves the way to his own destruction. One who does not walk the path of dharma cannot take even one step towards spiritual liberation.

The scriptures declare, '*Tat śṛṣṭvā tadēva anupraviśat*'—'Having created the universe, he entered into it' (*Taittirīya Upaniṣad*, 2.6). In other words, God is both the cause of creation and creation itself. Or, as Amma says, Creator and creation are not separate. Because dharma sustains the world, the nature of dharma is also divine. Dharma being God's creation, He is responsible for reinstating it whenever it declines. That is why, in each age, God incarnates to restore the balance of society. The avatārs and Gurus of that age instruct us on contemporary dharma.

Sanātana Dharma teaches us to follow moral values. For example, we are taught, *'satyam vada, dharmam cara'*—'Speak the truth. Follow the path of dharma.' When we fail to follow these precepts, morality declines and unrighteousness flourishes rampantly. In the bhajan '*Sadgurō Pāhimām,*' the poet writes '*satyam dharmatte nayicciḍēṇam*'—'Truth ought to lead dharma.' If we can maintain the awareness that God knows every one of our thoughts and actions, we will not do wrong. There will be no violence, theft or lying.

Once a girl in fourth grade asked Amma, "Amma, in the *Trēta Yuga*, Rāma incarnated to kill Rāvaṇa. In the *Dwāpara Yuga*, Kṛṣṇa incarnated to kill Kamsa. Who have you come to kill?"

Amma laughed loudly and said, "Amma has not come to kill anyone. But there are many demons in the minds of my children—the demons of ego. When these demons surface, Amma will eradicate them, and thus kill the ego."

To remove these demons or *adharmic* (unrighteous) elements, we need to cultivate qualities like patience and compassion. That is why God took the form of a mother.

Amma says that Śrī Kṛṣṇa's every action was rooted firmly in dharma. He also tried to make every person, both righteous and unrighteous, fit for God-realization and tried to cultivate dharmic consciousness in them. However, people like Kamsa were so completely identified with their ego that they could not walk the righteous path. Hence, the Lord had no choice but to get rid of them. He thus stopped adharma from flourishing further. But such is divine grace and mercy that he also liberated the wrongdoers.

Consider the following mantras from the *Lalitā Sahasranāma* (thousand names of the Divine Mother):

ōm cidagnikuṇḍa sambhūtāyai namaḥ
ōm dēvakārya samudyatāyai namaḥ

> Salutations to the Divine Mother, who was born in the fire-pit of pure consciousness.
> Salutations to the Divine Mother, who is intent on fulfilling the wishes of the gods. (4 – 5)

The Divine Mother emerged from the fire-pit of pure consciousness to help the gods. Who are these gods? They are the divine forces within us that inspire us to act selflessly. The Divine is none other than our own *ātma-śakti,* the power of our soul, which can free it from the clutches of the senses. Awakening this spiritual potential, which is lying dormant within us, is the only real solution for the problems of society. When Amma awakens our intellect, we will perceive the truth—*satyam*. When she acts through us, our actions will become auspicious—*śivam*. When she dawns in our heart, we will perceive beauty—*sundaram*. This is why God is seen as satyam-śivam-sundaram.

Swāmī Vivēkānanda said that spirituality does not mean retiring to a cave or forest and sitting there with eyes closed. The spiritual life ought to be a life based on compassion for our fellow beings. He declared he did not believe in any religion that could not appease the hunger of a starving person or wipe away the tears of the destitute. Swāmī Vivēkānanda reinterpreted the tradition of *sannyāsa* (renunciation) in terms of service to the world and compassion for all beings.

Amma exemplifies this ideal. Her darśan is an expression of the highest dharma: seeing God in one and all and receiving them as such. Amma's life is like the proverbial incense stick that burns itself out while spreading its fragrance. She accepts our negative tendencies, so that we may experience our own divine nature.

Amma has also reinstated the noble *Gurukula* tradition, one of the pillars of the ancient Indian culture. Simply put, a Gurukula is a school run by a Guru. It aims to uplift and inspire the disciples to rise to the level of the Guru. Amṛtapuri is Amma's Gurukula. What Amma does through each and every one of her actions is to awaken our *vivēka buddhi* (faculty of discernment), i.e. our inner Guru.

To awaken our inner wisdom, Amma has bequeathed to us many gems from the ancient tradition of *upāsana* (worship), including *mānasa pūjā* (worship through visualization), *arcana* (chanting of divine names) and *swādhyāya* (scriptural study). Thanks to Amma's efforts, the *Lalitā Sahasranāma* is today being chanted in temples and homes all over the world. Amma has nurtured young children by initiating *Bālakēndra* classes to develop good values in them. Similarly, chapters of the *Amrita Yuva Dharmadhara* (AYUDH) have been started all over the world to promote spirituality among youth. In these ways, Amma is guiding everyone based on age and maturity.

I first heard about Amma in a *Bālakēndra* class that taught Amma's bhajans and teachings. Nevertheless, I did not accept Amma as my God or Guru. But after attending the Kozhikode Brahmasthānam temple programs, my family members and I started to worship Amma. This happened after my younger brother died from snakebite when he was six years old. Our house was situated where the old Camuṇḍēśwarī *sarpakkāvu* had been located.[18] Tipu Sultan, the Indian Muslim ruler of the Kingdom of Mysore, had ordered its destruction. We used to see snakes in and around our courtyard. We performed pūjās in

---

18 *Camuṇḍēśwarī is a fierce form of the Goddess. A sarpakkāvu is a sacred grove where snakes are worshipped.*

different temples to protect ourselves from them, in vain. But as soon my mother performed a *Rāhu pūjā* at Amma's Kozhikode Brahmasthānam temple, the snakes stopped bothering us. Amma thus became our family savior. We placed her photo on our altar, lit the lamp twice a day, chanted the *Lalitā Sahasranāma* daily, and sang bhajans every evening.

I saw Amma for the first time when I was in 8th grade. Thereafter, she became the focus of my life. When I was in 10th grade, I visited the āśram and wanted to stay there. I tried to understand and follow the āśram discipline.

Amma's grace has always been with us. If anyone tried to obstruct our *sādhana* (spiritual practices), he or she would face the consequences soon enough. Once, while my sister and I were doing our morning arcana in front of the altar, our elder brother locked us inside. He opened it only an hour later, after my parents scolded him. Later that day, he told my mother that he was not feeling well. He came down with chickenpox. After this incident, he never interfered with our sādhana. Swāmī Dhyānāmṛtānanda Puri began to conduct satsaṅg-and-bhajan programs at our home. People who had been against Amma or had never bothered to learn more about her started to attend these programs.

Even though I was still quite young, my father gave me the freedom to engage in āśram-related activities such as bhajans, Bālakēndra classes, *Amrita Kuṭumbam* (local satsaṅgs), and AYUDH programs. When I was in pre-university, my sister shifted to the āśram. My older brothers feared that I might also take up the monastic life. Fortunately, my parents were supportive.

Once, when I wanted to attend Amma's public program in Mysore, my brother stopped me. But when he saw how sad I was, he accompanied me to Mysore. By the time we reached, darśan had already started. I sat down in the last row of the hall. When darśan was about to end, Amma asked a few brahmacāriṇīs to check if everyone had received darśan. A brahmacāriṇī approached me and asked if I had received darśan. When I said no, she took me to Amma.

Amma asked me, "Daughter, what do you want?"

I asked, "Amma, can I get a mantra?"

Amma said that she would give me one during the Dēvī Bhāva darśan the next day. Amma wore a beautiful cream-colored sari that reminded me of Saraswatī, the Goddess of Learning and the Arts. That evening, Amma gave me a mantra.

After I completed my degree, I wanted to do a course in computer science near Amṛtapuri to be close to the āśram. But because my sister had used a similar ruse and never returned home, my family members did not allow me to go. I then joined a government institute 40 kilometers away from the āśram. After the exams, I was assigned to teach in the same high school I had studied. After another four months, I found a job in a school near the Edappad satsaṅg.

One day, I met a *sannyāsi* from Chottanikkara. He spoke about his experience of going for Amma's darśan and of receiving a mantra from her. He told me, "Isn't it time to stop being childish? If you get the chance to be with Amma, you should not miss it. Stay in the āśram! It may take many lifetimes to get that chance again."

I went to see Amma. During darśan, I asked her if I could stay in the āśram. Amma said, "You're my daughter. You can stay."

Two days later, I asked Amma what *sēvā* (selfless service) I should do. Amma said, "I can't let you stay here! Where were you before this?" When I told her about my teaching job, she said, "Go back to the school immediately! You have abandoned your students."

I said, "If Amma makes a *saṅkalpa* (resolve), the school will find someone to replace me."

Amma said, "Your family members will create problems if you stay here. Go back home!"

I said, "I will not go back home or go to school!" Amma did not say anything.

The next day, I resolved to join the Sri Sarada Math, the women's wing of the Ramakrishna Math. I took an oath that I would keep Amma as my Guru. "Amma is within me," I thought, "I don't need her photo to meditate on her."

I decided to see Amma one last time and seek her permission before leaving forever. When I went for darśan, I was thinking, "Why doesn't Amma allow me to stay here? She allows so many people to stay. Maybe Amma does not want me!" I started crying.

When she saw me crying, Amma turned to the person beside her and said, "I've already allowed her to stay here. Why is she crying?"

Two days later, Bri. Bhāvāmṛtājī asked me to serve in the *pañcakarma*[19] treatments department. I was happy to do so. I used to see a Western woman massaging Amma and would think how lucky she was to be able to touch Amma and be in her presence constantly. Chanting the *Lalitā Sahasranāma* during the sēvā brought me even closer to Amma. I wanted to learn the scriptures, but unfortunately, did not have time

---

19 *An Ayurvedic cleansing and rejuvenating treatment.*

for either meditation or scriptural classes. Amma gave me a solution. She said, "Amma is present in all the women who come for treatment. See all of them as Amma. That way, whenever you're doing sēvā, you'll always be thinking of Amma. That's meditation." Amma added that I should listen to recordings of scriptural classes and take notes.

Once, during the sēvā, I accidentally spilled hot medicinal paste on my right hand. Fearing that I would be scolded if I told someone, I kept mum. It was a Tuesday morning. By the afternoon, I felt as if my hand was burning. When I went to collect lunch prasād from Amma, I raised my left hand to receive it, but Amma did not hand me the prasād until I took it with my right hand. She then held the plate of prasād and looked intently at my right hand. She did not say anything. After some time, the burning sensation subsided. After that incident, I became more alert in my sēvā.

Twelve years have passed since Amma asked me to take notes of the scripture classes. Recently, she told me to write a satsaṅg on each topic. She even guided me on how to write a satsaṅg. She said, "The whole world is plunged in sorrow. It is your duty to save them!" When I told her that I was conducting Bālakēndra classes for children, Amma asked, "Then who will teach the elders?"

In my first room darśan, Amma had said, "I will make you lift a mountain" (meaning, she will make me do the impossible). It was only after I went to Kovai in Tamil Nadu to perform pūjās in the Brahmasthānam temple there that I understood the significance of Amma's words. Together with other brahmacāriṇīs, we had to conduct hōmas, sing bhajans and even give satsaṅgs in Tamil. By Amma's grace, everything went very well.

The truth is one. Without discriminating against anyone, let us all do what we can to serve the world humbly.

22

Dedication to Dharma

Br. Sumēdhāmṛta Caitanya

Amma has said, "Often, my children don't remember the spiritual principles I teach but they can recall the stories I narrated." Stories can convey profound spiritual truths. Here is one such tale.

There once lived a bull elephant named Paṭṭāmbi Nārāyaṇan. It had gained a reputation for being a killer, as it had slain more than 40 men. No mahout dared to go near it. Paṭṭāmbi Nārāyaṇan was sold to a man, who paid an advance of ₹50,000; the rest was to be paid upon delivery. But who would deliver Paṭṭāmbi Nārāyaṇan to him?

That was when news came of a fearless mahout named Pāṇan Nārāyaṇan. Though only four-and-a-half feet tall, his reputation as tamer of tuskers was outsized. He was summoned and asked if he could deliver Paṭṭāmbi Nārāyaṇan to the buyer. At first, Pāṇan Nārāyaṇan was intimidated by the task entrusted to him, as he had also heard about Paṭṭāmbi Nārāyaṇan. But he did not let his fear show. Instead, he said, "If you pay me ₹5,000, I'll take on the assignment." In those days, the maximum daily wage he could expect was ₹25.

The buyer agreed; he had no other choice. Pāṇan Nārāyaṇan was taken to Paṭṭāmbi Nārāyaṇan, who was trumpeting in rage, as if raring to kill. Seeing Pāṇan Nārāyaṇan, it hurled a three-and-a-half feet long coconut leaf at him, knocking him down. The mahout slowly got up and smoked a couple of *bīḍis.*[20] He then glared murderously at the elephant. Sensing that the man was no longer fearful, the elephant began to retreat in fear.

Pāṇan Nārāyaṇan yelled, "Left!" Paṭṭāmbi Nārāyaṇan moved to the left. "Right!" The elephant moved to the right. "Sit!" The elephant sat. "Stand!" It stood up.

Pāṇan Nārāyaṇan was thus able to subdue Paṭṭāmbi Nārāyaṇan eventually and became his mahout. When someone asked him how he succeeded, he said, "In Paṭṭāmbi Nārāyaṇan's mind, he is four-and-a-half-feet tall whereas Pāṇan Nārāyaṇan is ten-and-a-half-feet high. So, it continues to obey me."

Likewise, we are all mahouts of our minds, which have gone on many rampages and done much harm. Just as elephants like to graze in the forest and bathe in soil but do not enjoy being put to work, our mind does not like meditation, scriptural study and other disciplines that the Guru prescribes. We must curb this resistance and cultivate an attitude of surrender to the Guru's instructions. Only then can we tame the Paṭṭāmbi Nārāyaṇan of our mind. But if our love for and faith in the Guru diminishes, our spiritual practices will become lax. Then our rogue minds will gain strength. Before we know it, we will become the next victim of our own mind.

Amma is the perfect mahout of human tuskers. She came into the world silently. The *Aṣṭōttaram* (108 attributes) in her honor say, *'ōm niśśabda jananīgarbha nirggamādbhuta karmaṇē namaḥ'* — 'Salutations to Amma, who miraculously emerged silently from her mother's womb' (24). In doing so, Amma

---

20 Cheap cigarettes made of unprocessed tobacco wrapped in leaves.

proclaimed aloud the message of Sage Dakṣiṇāmūrti[21] to the world: that the Guru is essentially silent and that in silence lies the exposition of the highest knowledge: *mauna vyākhyā prakaṭita parabrahmatattvam* (*Dakṣiṇāmūrti Stōtram*, 1).

Amma was completely aware of her divine nature from birth. She wants us also to realize that divinity is our true nature, too. She guides us on how to connect with our inner Amma, the abode of silence. To attain this sacred realm, we must follow *dharma*, the path of righteousness.

We are often not clear about what is right and what is wrong. But if we carefully observe Amma's actions and follow her teachings, we can learn how to live peacefully and happily.

I first saw Amma in 1989, a day after *Tiruvōṇam.*[22] That day, I asked her if I could stay in the āśram. She looked at me and said, "Think deeply about it."

After this, I started visiting the āśram three times a month for a while. Earlier, I had been obsessed with volleyball and movies. Playing volleyball had also been a good source of income for me. But as I got closer to Amma, I began to lose interest in both. Friends began to say of me, "He used to be a smart kid, but after meeting Amma, he has changed!"

Amma sings a bhajan named *'Kālī Mahēśwariyē.'* One of the lines in it is, "I will chant your name until I reach your world." My situation was like that. Having developed a taste for spirituality, all I wanted to do was to be with Amma. When I could not visit the āśram, I would fast and remain in silence.

---

21 *An aspect of Lord Śiva, the Destroyer in the Hindu Trinity. Also considered the first Guru.*

22 *The last day of Ōṇam, which is Kerala's biggest festival, occurring in the month of Ciṅṅam* (August – September).

Meeting Amma awoke a long-buried desire to lead the life of a monk. When I was in third grade, I saw a movie about Ādi Śaṅkarācārya[23] that attracted me to the monastic life. Although I did not know anything about monasticism then, I was nonetheless fascinated by it. I started observing fasts and felt sad that I had not been born during Ādi Śaṅkarācārya's time.

After graduating from college, I came to Amṛtapuri to seek Amma's permission to join the āśram, but she was about to leave for a tour abroad. Bombay-*acchan*, who was in charge of accommodation then, said, "Amma told me to send visitors back home. But I won't ask you to leave. I'll let you decide for yourself." As it did not seem right to violate Amma's instructions, I left.

The period that followed was rough. My father was diagnosed with cancer. I wanted to look after him, but he insisted that I further my studies. Unable to ask Amma what to do, I went to Karnataka to study. My father died before I finished my degree.

Not long after, by Amma's grace alone, I was able to work briefly in her school in Kodungalloor. Although I was still keen on leading a monastic life, I had worldly obligations to fulfill. I needed to support my mother, who was still grieving. I had several interactions with Amma about coming to live in the āśram.

Finally, in 1995, Amma allowed me to become a resident of Amṛtapuri. She said, "Go home, inform your family, and then go and teach at the Kodungalloor Amrita Vidyalayam (school)."

When I informed my mother, she asked me, "I've seen senior swāmīs leave the āśram. Will you be able to endure everything?"

I told her, "Mother, we don't stop traveling just because we have seen accidents on the way, do we?"

---

23 Saint and chief proponent of the Advaita (non-dual) philosophy.

Although it took me six years to join the āśram, the final decision was quick. I just knew that āśram life was all that I wanted, and the time was right to dedicate myself to the ultimate goal of life.

We all face dilemmas in life and must decide on the right course of action. When Arjuna sought Kṛṣṇa's advice, the Lord spoke to him about the higher purpose of life — the non-dual realization of Brahman (the Supreme) — but told Arjuna to fight the war. Hearing this, Arjuna said, "Instead of confusing me, please tell me decisively what will bring me fortune and prosperity." He was like a 10th grader asking his mother, "After telling me to aim for a PhD, why are you telling me to prepare for my 10th-grade exams?" The mother patiently explains that to get a PhD, he would first have to clear the lower grades.

Arjuna told Lord Kṛṣṇa that he wanted to become a monk, but the Lord told him to fight. This is because Kṛṣṇa knew that Arjuna's nature was that of a warrior and not an ascetic. Knowing the nature of Uddhava, Kṛṣṇa's friend and adviser, the Lord advised him to walk the path of *jñāna* (Self-inquiry).

In the *Bhagavad Gītā*, it is said:

> *śrēyān swadharmō viguṇaḥ paradharmāt swanuṣṭhitāt*
> *swadharmē nidhanam śrēyaḥ paradharmō bhayāvahaḥ*
> Better to do one's duty, even if it be imperfect, than that of another, even if that be perfect. Better to die while doing one's duty; the duty of another person is fraught with danger. (3.35)

Hinduism acknowledges war as a necessary means to check evil and uphold dharma. The role of a *kṣatriya*, a warrior, is to protect his country and people. To dispel Arjuna's illusion and remove his attachments to what is transient, Lord Kṛṣṇa guides him to doing his duty (*swadharma*). He teaches him to perform it as a *yajña*, an offering to God. What inspires us to do right is dharmic, especially if it is sanctioned by the scriptures.

Dharma comes from the Sanskrit root '*dhṛ,*' which means 'to hold or support.' It involves discriminating between right and wrong and upholding the former. The sense of what is right is honed by the study of the scriptures.

Dharma can be understood in different ways. There is personal dharma, which includes understanding the do's and don'ts, as expounded in *Manusmṛti,*[24] accepting both joy and sorrow with equanimity, exercising patience towards all creatures, having control over the mind, abstaining from stealing, maintaining internal and external purity, controlling one's senses, speaking the truth, and refraining from expressing anger.

There is also family dharma. We all play roles in the family, whether as brother/sister, son/daughter, father/mother, and husband/wife. We must perform our respective duties well.

Community or social dharma entails obeying the rules and conventions of society, and doing good to society.

National dharma encompasses patriotism, commitment to the nation, preserving its culture, maintaining traditional knowledge, and guarding its wealth and frontiers.

World dharma is a consciousness of the whole world as one family. The ancients of India called it "*vasudhaiva kuṭumbakam.*" Acting to promote global interests is honoring world dharma.

Amma has expressed these aspects of dharma right from her childhood. She gave up schooling for the sake of her family. She comforted troubled and suffering souls in society. Her presence

---

24 Ancient text on how society should be run.

and teachings are a source of national pride and pride in India's spiritual heritage. Above all, Amma embraces people from all walks of life, cultures and nationalities as her own children, thus expressing the ideal of vasudhaiva kuṭumbakam in the most tangible way.

Dharma can also be based on one's vocation or calling in life. Arjuna's was the *kṣatriya dharma*, the dharma of a warrior. The *Bhagavad Gītā* explains what this is:

> *śauryam tējō dhṛtirdākṣyam yuddhē cāpyapalāyanam*
> *dānam īśvara-bhāvaśca kṣatram karma svabhāvajam*
> Courage, brilliance, power, prowess in combat, never retreating from battle, generosity and leadership are the characteristic traits of kṣatriyas. (18.43)

Lord Kṛṣṇa adds, *"swakarmaṇā tam abhyarcya siddhim vindati mānavaḥ"* — "by worshipping God through one's duties, one attains perfection" (18.46). There is no greater *jñāna sādhana* (means of gaining spiritual knowledge) than this. For a kṣatriya, fighting to eradicate evil and establish goodness is dharma. If a warrior fights selflessly and without any attachment to the result, then he is freed from the clutches of karma and the *yuddha* (war) becomes a *yajña* (worship). This is the subtle, hidden essence of karma.

The *Mahābhārata* praises kṣatriya dharma as the highest dharma, for a kṣatriya protects humanity from harm. Rulers must govern the country and protect the people in accordance with the dictates of dharma. When they do so, peace and prosperity will prevail, as indicated by the following peace invocation:

> *ōm swastiḥ prajābhyaḥ paripālayantām*

nyāyēna mārgēṇa mahīm mahīśāḥ
gō-brāhmaṇēbhyaḥ śubhamastu nityam
lōkāh samastāḥ sukhinō bhavantu
May people be prosperous and protected.
May the rulers govern righteously.
May animals and the wise ever do well.
May all beings everywhere be peaceful.

If one's actions are unrighteous or if one engages in *paradharma* (the duties of others), a conflict will arise, and one will never reach the ultimate goal of life: Self-realization.

Swāmī Vivēkānanda says, "The essence of all morality is to do good to others... be unselfish." One can only be selfless when one is detached. In the *Bhagavad Gītā*, we see that Arjuna was disturbed and confused because of his attachment to his loved ones.

It can be said that the solution to all problems in life is awareness. Although Arjuna had studied the Vēdas, he became deluded at the most important juncture in his life, owing to his attachment. If such is the state of a learned and redoubtable warrior, what to say of mere mortals like us!

During the Mahābhārata War, when Bhīṣma, the commander-in-chief of the Kaurava army, blew his conch to announce the commencement of the war, the first to respond on the Pāṇḍavas' side was Lord Kṛṣṇa; he sounded his holy conch. The truth was, the Lord was the unofficial commander of the Pāṇḍavas. By virtue of his intelligence, power and strategy, he orchestrated the downfall of all the great warriors on the Kaurava side. Truly, dharma always concurs with the will of God.

For this reason, it is best to follow the advice of *mahātmās* (spiritually illumined souls), for they are one with the Divine. It has been my experience that when I act without consulting Amma, I create a mess! But when I seek her advice, I benefit from her wisdom and foresight.

In February 2020, I planned a program to be conducted in April that year. It was supposed to be a big event, and around 2,000 people were expected to attend. When I went for darśan in February, somehow, I felt that I ought to ask Amma about this program. At that time, the coronavirus had not spread widely in India. Amma's spontaneous response was, "No, son, don't conduct this program. Even Amma is not going to conduct programs now."

Over the next month, the epidemic became a global pandemic. Had I proceeded with my plans, which would have included making advance payments, the results would have been disastrous. The scriptwriter alone knows how the story will unfold.

Swāmī Rāmakṛṣṇānanda once said, "Amma places her trust in us. That's why she sends us out into the world as her representatives. But we must look within to see if we truly have total faith in her."

I'm reminded of a friend, Tommy Matthew, who used to play volleyball with me when I was in college and who later became an all-rounder in the Indian Volleyball team. I come across an interview with him recently. He was asked, "While training under coach Shyam Sundar Rao, you were the one who was punished most often. Seeing his harsh treatment, many other players wanted to quit. How did you endure such treatment?"

Tommy's reply was insightful, "Coach Shyam Sundar Rao has received both the Arjuna Award and the Dronacharya Award. The minimum height set for players was 190 centimeters. Though I was only 187 centimeters tall, Coach Shyam Sundar selected me into the team. I was convinced that he had seen something in me."

Tommy continued, "When he used to punish me, all I could see was a deeply committed and concerned teacher who wanted to bring out the best in me, something he alone could see. Moreover, I had an intense desire to achieve excellence in volleyball. I was convinced that there was no better opportunity than this, and that no one other than him could help me. Whenever I was punished, I would focus on what I could learn in the process. His faith in me was justified eventually. I emerged as the best all-rounder and back-row attacker in the Indian junior and senior teams. It is only because of his faith in me and his perseverance that I have a bright future in sports today."

If such are the efforts a sports coach makes to create a sportsman of repute, how much more committed a Guru must be to help us fulfill the highest goal of life. On our part, we must look within to see if we have the dedication to the goal. We must ask ourselves if we have the patience and forbearance to stay on the path with Amma until we attain God. She alone can give us the strength needed to reach her holy abode. To earn that grace, we must become deserving. Let us try to cultivate it through sincere effort and an attitude of dedication and surrender.

23
The Blossoming of Knowledge

Bri. Puṇyāmṛta Caitanyā

In the *Bhagavad Gītā*, Lord Kṛṣṇa speaks of the difference between a *jñānī* (Self-realized being) and an *ajñānī* (unenlightened):

> *yā niśā sarvabhūtānām tasyām jāgarti samyamī*
> *yasyām jāgrati bhūtāni sā niśā paśyatō munēḥ*
> What all beings consider day is the night of ignorance to the wise, and what all creatures consider night is day for the introspective sage. (2.69)

Most people abide in a world of delusion, which gives only temporary pleasure. The jñānī gives little importance to this illusory reality. Having realized his own true nature, he sees the divine consciousness in everyone and everything. His experience is "*īśāvāsyam idam sarvam*" — "a world enveloped by God" (*Īśāvāsya Upaniṣad*, 1). He cannot see anyone or anything as separate from himself, and therefore feels no hatred towards anyone:

> *yastu sarvāṇi bhūtāni ātmanyēvānupaśyati*
> *sarvabhūtēṣu cātmānam tatō na vijugupsatē*
> One who sees everything in the Self and the Self in everything thereafter feels no hatred for anything. (*Īśāvāsya Upaniṣad*, 6)

The Self refers to pure consciousness, which empowers and enables the ears to hear, the mind to reflect, the mouth to speak, the eyes to see, and the life energy (*prāṇa*) to move. The *Kēnōpaniṣad* points out that we cannot know the Self by these instruments. This teaching is encapsulated in '*Kātinnu kātāyi,*' a bhajan Amma sings:

> *kātinnu kātāyi manassin manassāyi kaṇṇinnu kaṇṇāyi vilasunnorammē*
> *prāṇannu prāṇan ni tanneyallō jīvannu jīvan ninnuṇmayallō*
> O Mother, who shines as the Ear of the ear, Mind of the mind, and Eye of the eye,
> You are the Life of life and your being is the Life of the living.

The seers of antiquity called us "*amṛtasya putrāḥ*" — "the children of immortality." Amma addresses us as "the form of love, the form of the Self." '*Ōmkāra Divya Poruḷē,*' a poetic rendering of Amma's teachings, begins with the following lines:

> Come quickly, my darling children, who are the essence of Ōm.
> Dispel all sorrow, remove the impurities from the mind, and become one with Ōm.

'Ōm' is a symbol of the Supreme. Amma perceives that supreme consciousness within us and, so, lovingly addresses us as the essence of Ōm. She also urges us to become like innocent children with an expansive mind, for only a child can grow. True innocence and expansiveness mean an absence of mental impurities such as anger, jealousy or pride. These *vāsanās* (latent tendencies) prevent us from knowing the Self. The root cause of ignorance is desire, which eclipses Self-knowledge just as smoke conceals fire or dark clouds cover the sun. Once desire leaves us, all other vāsanās will drop away, and we will be liberated from the cycle of birth and death.

However, we cannot rid ourselves completely of desires and other vāsanās through our own efforts. Only a Guru can. Amma smooths our rough edges by putting us in situations that cause friction, in the same way as stones in a tumbler rub against each other, causing their sharp edges to be worn away. Amma says, "This āśram is a *Kurukṣētra* (battlefield). One who wins the battle here will succeed anywhere in the world."

As long as we remain ignorant of our real nature, we will continue to be reborn. Once we gain that ultimate knowledge, we will never again be reborn, either in this world or elsewhere. This is what spiritual liberation is.

Lord Kṛṣṇa tells Arjuna, "Just as fire reduces wood to ash, the effulgence of spiritual knowledge eradicates the consequences of all action" (*Bhagavad Gītā*, 4.37). In the next verse, he tells Arjuna, "*na hi jñānēna sadṛśam pavitramiha vidyatē*" — "In this world, there is nothing as purifying as divine knowledge."

How can we get rid of our ignorance? We must turn our attention inwards. We are naturally inclined to be distracted by the outer world because our senses are designed that way. Amma says that we have come on a picnic to this world; once it is over, we must return home. We came from God and to Him must we return. Spiritual life is an inward journey.

Once, a Guru knocked on his disciple's door. Knowing who it was, the disciple said "O Guru, please enter."

"I cannot open the door from the outside. You must open it for me from the inside."

These words have a deeper meaning. The Guru embodies supreme knowledge. Only when she becomes enshrined in the disciple's heart can supreme knowledge dawn in her.

Once, Amma came to our rooms early in the morning and knocked on our doors to find out who had woken up in time to go for the morning *arcana* and who were still sleeping. No doubt, her action was also meant to make us aware of her true purpose in our lives.

In order to learn anything, we need a teacher. For example, to learn how to play the flute well, we must be guided by an expert flautist. Likewise, on the spiritual path, we need a Guru to help us attain knowledge of our true Self.

Knowledge is of two kinds: book knowledge and experiential knowledge. If we study the scriptures, we can gain book knowledge. But only the Guru's grace can give us experiential knowledge. Self-knowledge is what elevates man to Godhood. The lotus blooms only in the presence of the sun. Similarly, the flower of ultimate knowledge will blossom only in the presence of a Guru. The *Kaṭhōpaniṣad* says, "Arise and awake. Having come into the presence of Self-realized spiritual masters, take refuge in them. The wise say that the path to the Self is arduous" (1.3.14).

I was a student when I first met Amma in 1987. At the time, I was not interested in spirituality or life in an āśram. After finishing my degree, I came to the āśram to enroll in a computer course in the Amrita Institute of Computer Technology (AICT) in Puthiyakavu. There were both short-term (3 – 6 months) and long-term (one-year) courses being offered. I enrolled in a one-year course, intending to return home after completing it.

However, during that year, I became attached to Amma and found āśram life entirely to my liking. I would go for darśan, attend bhajans, and participate in *sēvā* (selfless service) activities on most nights. One day, when I went for darśan, Amma told me to sit beside her. I innocently sat down beside her on her *pīṭham* (seat of the Guru). Seeing this, Amma and the others started laughing. I looked at them, not knowing why they were laughing. I held Amma's left hand and snuggled against her soft body. Amma continued to give darśan. But not once did she take her hand away or ask me to move. I lost all awareness of my surroundings. For quite some time, I sat holding her hand, leaning against her. Eventually, I got up quietly and sat on the floor beside her. In my ignorance, I did not know that when Amma tells someone to sit beside her, it does not mean to sit on her pīṭham but next to it.

I did not want to leave Amma and return home when my course ended. I went for darśan and asked her if I may stay in the āśram. Amma answered, "Not now. Go and get a job!"

Instead of leaving, I waited for Dēvī Bhava darśan and asked her again if I could stay. Amma said, "Daughter, there's no space to stay even for those who are already here. So, you must go home."

When I returned home, I decided to further my studies and returned to the āśram after two days to seek Amma's blessings. However, when I went for darśan, instead of seeking her blessings for my studies, I found myself asking her, yet again, "May I stay here?"

Amma said, "Daughter, this place looks cool from the outside, but inside, it's very hot!"

Even after hearing this, I did not return home. It was time for Amma's foreign tour. A few days before her departure, she gave darśan to āśram residents. I knew that only residents were allowed to stay in the āśram when Amma was not there. I decided to go for yet another darśan. As I stood in the darśan queue, I started praying fervently, "O Amma, please let me stay!" This time, when I asked her, she gave me permission.

I started reflecting on Amma's words: "It is cool from the outside but hot inside." I realized that when Amma tries to eradicate our deep-rooted vāsanās, we must endure what is akin to an almost unbearable heat. The āśram environment is an arena to wage battle with our vāsanās.

That said, just moving into the āśram is not enough. Amma is constantly trying to awaken those among us who are sunk in the slumber of ignorance. Sometimes, she wears a mask of anger to rouse us. Seeing this, we must not run away in fear but hold on to her feet tightly, for we can attain true knowledge only by Amma's grace.

Once a devotee asked Amma, "You can bestow Self-realization on everyone, if you so desire. Why don't you do so?"

Amma said, "My conscience is like a weighing scale. On one pan is Amma's grace. To balance the scale, my children should put forth effort in equal measure." She says that acting with humility draws grace.

Several candidates attended a job interview. After their interviews, they discussed among themselves the answers to the questions. Only one person had answered all the answers correctly. He was confident that he would be selected for the job. But another candidate was appointed. Disappointed, the first candidate decided to find out why he had not been selected. The interviewer explained, "Do you remember how you entered the room? You kicked the door open!"

The candidate protested, "I had to because I was carrying files in my hands!"

"The candidate who was selected was also carrying files, but he kept them aside and opened the door with his hands. We do not kick the objects we respect."

It was the humility of the second candidate that earned him the grace of the interviewer.

Amma says that we should not hurt anyone in any way. There is an aura around us that absorbs each one of our thoughts, words and actions. Good words and deeds will brighten the aura around us, but when we hurt someone, the pain he or she feels will rebound on us and darken the aura around us. This, in turn, will block the flow of grace.

Once, a disciple went to his master, confessed that he was prone to getting angry quickly, and asked for a solution. The master gave him a piece of paper and said, "Tear it into as many tiny pieces as possible and bring them back to me." The disciple did as he was told and brought the torn pieces to the master, who said, "Now, restore the paper to its original state." The disciple could not. The master said, "The words we utter and the actions we do are like these shreds of paper. We can never undo the damage done. Therefore, speak and act with utmost attentiveness."

It is said that the disciple must strive to please the Guru by his actions. His attitude of self-sacrifice and surrender will draw the grace of the Guru. Amma says, "I keep flowing like a river. If a hole is dug nearby, water will naturally fill it." Our good words and deeds are like the hole on the riverbank.

I remember an incident that happened many years ago. It was past midnight. Amma was standing below her room and talking to two brahmacārīs. Suddenly, she closed her eyes. When she opened them moments later, they were filled with tears. She said softly, "One of my sons (in another branch) started working in the morning and only just finished his work. Though he's tired, he has not gone to bed. Instead, in obedience to my words, he is sitting down to meditate. His sacrifice and surrender fill my heart with compassion towards him." Amma knows each and every one of our thoughts and actions, wherever we may be.

Knowledge dawns only in a pure heart. Otherwise, accumulating scriptural knowledge would be like pouring milk into a dirty vessel; the milk will turn sour. In the *Vivēkacūḍāmaṇi*, Ādi Śaṅkarācārya says, *"Cittasya śuddhaye karma"* — "Selfless action cleanses the mind" (11). That is why Amma encourages her children to engage in sēvā, so that we can become worthy of receiving the highest wisdom.

How should we do sēvā? Amma says that the attitude behind the act is more important than the action itself. She sees only the sincerity and faith with which we perform each action. We might make mistakes. Even so, Amma gives more importance to attitude than to skill. Sometimes, while doing sēvā, we might become defeated by circumstances. This was my experience. The only reason I prevailed was Amma's love alone, and not my skill, devotion or knowledge of the scriptures. She understood my helplessness and showered me with immense love and compassion. Amma said, "Because you're here, you had to undergo only a tiny fraction of what you would have had to experience in the world outside." Her reassuring words gave me the strength to persevere.

Amma says that if we perform our actions as worship, the outcome will be sanctified, like *prasād* (consecrated offering).

She says that if we can make each one of our actions an offering to the Lord, we will attain spiritual liberation.

To illustrate, Amma narrates the following story. One of the disciples in a Gurukula[25] was entrusted with the job of maintaining the store. Late one night, the Guru saw a light in this disciple's room. When he went in, he saw the disciple tallying the month's expenses. As soon as the Guru moved close to him, the disciple was able to finalize the accounts. He shouted in relief, "Finally!" It was then that he noticed the Guru. He hurriedly stood up and explained, "There was a difference of 50 *paisa* in the accounts. I was finally able to account for it." The Guru's heart swelled with love and compassion for his disciple, who worked with such sincerity and faith. He embraced his disciple and blessed him with the knowledge of the Self.

It is said that when we truly prostrate with all our heart at the Guru's feet, we will be able to see her effulgent form clearly in our hearts. In her compassion, she will then grant us liberation. We have reached the sacred abode of the Guru. May our hearts become pure and worthy of her grace so that true knowledge blossoms in our hearts.

---

25 The kula *(clan) of a Guru, a Gurukula is a traditional school where students would stay with the Guru for the entire duration of their studies.*

24

Holding on Tightly

Bri. Samagītāmṛta Caitanyā

Many years ago, I saw āśram residents gathered around the tank near Amma's room. When I went there, I saw Amma standing beside the tank, pushing people, one by one, into the water. Then Amma jumped in and joined them. I noticed that she was standing at the shallow end, holding people up at arm's length by their hair. Amma explained that if we want to save someone from drowning, we should hold them while keeping a safe distance from them. Or else, they will grab us in panic and pull us down, and both will drown!

Doesn't the same principle apply to any situation in life? We cannot help others unless we keep a safe distance from the situation. Amma says that we should develop the attitude of witnessing. We can neither control situations or individuals nor expect satisfaction, happiness and security from things outside us. But we can rise above any situation by developing the ability to see everything as a witness. This is the essence of the *Bhagavad Gītā*.

I first met Amma when I was in the 8th standard. Amma was leaving for her first World Tour on May 14th, 1987. I accompanied my grandfather to the airport to see her. As Amma came out of the VIP lounge, she stopped to talk to him and asked about his welfare. Amma also looked at me. I still recall that mesmerizing look.

Grandfather used to conduct *saptāhams* (seven-day recitations) of the *Śrīmad Bhāgavatam* every year. In one of these saptāhams, Grandfather met Ōṭṭūr Uṇṇi Nanpūtirippāḍ, the composer of Amma's *Aṣṭōttaram* (108 attributes), and invited him to conduct a *Bhāgavata* saptāham at home. Ōṭṭūr Uṇṇi Nanpūtirippāḍ agreed and thus the two of them became close. Later, Grandfather accompanied Ōṭṭūr Uṇṇi Nanpūtirippāḍ to Amṛtapuri for the first time in 1985. On that day, Amma told Grandfather, "In future, your grandchildren will come here." Her words were prophetic.

Grandfather told us that Amma was an incarnation of Lord Kṛṣṇa. She blessed our family by staying in my grandfather's house three times. But as my father's job took us away from Kerala, we did not see Amma again until 1989. Finally, my father was transferred back to Kochi, and thus, we were able to spend all our weekends with Amma.

I used to worry about whether or not Amma would let me stay in the āśram and about whether I could live the āśram life. One Tuesday, when I went to collect prasād from Amma after meditation, she said, "You're neither on land nor in water!" I took that as a sign from Amma that I should commit to the āśram life. That way, I could move out of the water and onto the shore!

For years, I wore a gold chain with a locket of Guruvāyūrappan (a form of Lord Viṣṇu). I had stuck a picture of Amma on one side of the locket. One day, I thought, "Am I not wearing this necklace only because of the Amma sticker?" When I looked at the locket the next day, I realized that the sticker was missing!

This convinced me to remove the necklace. I saw this as another sign that I should choose the āśram life.

Another day, I saw a photo of Amma and some soap on my mat. I had no idea who had put them there. In the photo, Amma was standing with her arms outstretched as if she was trying to lift a child. She had a mischievous smile. Looking at it, I felt Amma was beckoning me to come into her arms. When I used that soap, made in the āśram, I felt a deep joy that I had never felt before. It made me feel that I belonged here. I went for darśan and asked Amma, "Amma, will you let me stay in the āśram?"

Amma said, "No! Definitely not! Your family members must agree."

I was distraught. I was sure that my parents would object, as my older sister had joined the āśram. But surprisingly, they did not. Father said, "Only Amma knows what is good for you. If she says yes, I will agree."

That year, when Amma called the brahmacāriṇīs for room darśan, I asked a senior brahmacāriṇī to ask Amma about me. She did and reported that Amma had said yes and that I should also go for the room darśan. I was overjoyed! I went for the room darśan in colored clothes. Amma said, "Daughter, from now on, wear only white."

I looked into Amma's eyes and sat still. Amma then asked, "Why are you so thin? Not eating?"

I said, "Amma, I don't like *kaññi* (rice gruel)."

"Then what do you like?"

"*Chapātī* (unleavened flatbread) and rice," I said.

I thought Amma would arrange this food for me. Instead, she lovingly said, "Take the rice from the kaññi first and then drink the water after that." Thus, Amma helped me take the first, baby steps on this path. The Guru comes down to our level and gently directs us towards God without causing any turmoil in us. In the *Bhagavad Gītā*, Lord Kṛṣṇa says,

> *na buddhi-bhēdam janayēd ajñānām karma-saṅginām*
> *jōṣayet sarva-karmāṇi vidvān yuktaḥ samācaran*
>
> The wise should not discompose the minds of ignorant people, who are attached to the fruits of their labors. Instead, they should encourage them to do all their work attentively. (3.26)

People act according to their innate nature. Most act only to fulfill their selfish interests. We learn to act selflessly only when our inner wisdom is awakened.

Once, there lived in a small village a milkman named Ashok. He was honest but unhappy. He could not find any contentment in life. One day, while returning home, he saw a *sannyāsi* (ordained monk) meditating. When the sannyāsi opened his eyes, Ashok asked him, "How can I attain happiness and contentment in my life?"

The sannyāsi pointed to a pond and asked Ashok to ask the fish in the pond. He said, "You'll get the answer from them."

Ashok did as he was told. One fish said, "Before I answer your question, please get me some water to drink!"

Ashok was surprised. "Why do you want water when you're already living in water?"

The fish said, "That's the answer to your question! All virtues are within us. We only have to awaken them!"

Whenever Amma entrusts us with some *sēvā* (selfless service), she aims to awaken the virtues dormant in us.

What is the right way to perform sēvā? Amma shows us through her actions. Once, a devotee asked Amma, "Why don't you take a break? You can go to a place like Hawaii. You can spend time relaxing on the beach."

Amma laughed loudly and said, "Son, don't you have a son? Suppose he falls sick and wants you by his side. Will you leave him to go sightseeing? Likewise, all of you are my children. I cannot leave you and sit idly somewhere else."

We must strive to do everything with utmost *śraddhā* (alertness) and *vivēka* (discernment). In addition, we must cultivate love and compassion towards all beings.

There once lived a carpenter named Chandu. He was hardworking and highly skilled. As he approached old age, he wanted to retire and spend the rest of his life with his children. He told his master about his decision. The master thought for a moment and said, "Chandu, I want a new house. Before you retire, would you please do all the woodwork for it?"

Chandu had never refused his master anything. So, he set out to work, but he did it half-heartedly. Instead of selecting hardwood, known for its solidity and longevity, Chandu used cheap and soft timber, which was not long-lasting. He worked without enthusiasm and sincerity.

When the house was complete, Chandu informed his master, who joyfully presented the keys to the new house to Chandu and said, "The house is for you!"

Chandu felt sharp pangs of guilt and regret for his carelessness. We can choose how we act in every situation in life. Amma says that we must perform every action with a worshipful attitude and accept the results with *prasāda-buddhi*, the feeling that whatever we receive is a gift from God. If we can dedicate every action to God, we will have the mental strength to accept any outcome, whether good or bad.

This reminds me of one of Amma's stories. It was *Tiruvōṇam*[26] in Vṛndāvan. Kṛṣṇa always gave gifts to the *gōpīs* (milkmaids). But this time, he told them to choose gifts for themselves. Rādhā arrived only after everyone else had taken their gifts and left. As a result, all she got was a little piece of blue cloth. One of the other gōpīs told her, "If only you'd come earlier, you'd have gotten better clothes."

Rādhā cheerfully said, "I consider myself blessed to have received this. After all, it's a gift from the Lord. Moreover, whenever I see the blue color, I'll remember the Lord."

Amma tells us these stories to awaken positive qualities like gratitude in us. She often says that nature is our mother and Guru, who is always trying to teach us selflessness. If we observe natural phenomena attentively, we will understand what Amma means. The sun provides us with light and heat. The full moonlight cools the mind. The stars awaken joy in us. The cool breeze awakens feelings of peace and fulfillment. Rains bathe nature and invigorate life. Trees provide us with fruit and shade. Flowers exude fragrance and a soothing beauty. Streams give us pure and refreshing water. Amma says that butterflies and rainbows live for a few moments, but they make us happy. All beings do their duties and live in harmony with nature, all beings but man, that is.

Amma finds ways to teach us, even when we are not physically with her. Sometimes, she guides devotees through dreams. Swāmī Amṛtātmānanda once recounted the story of a

---

26 Kerala's biggest festival, occurring in the month of Ciṅṅam (August *– September).*

sannyāsi, who used to perform austerities on the banks of the Ganges. When he fell into a state of spiritual confusion, Amma appeared to him in a dream and gave him guidance. He later came to see Amma in person.

Often, the Guru helps the disciples learn spiritual lessons through situations. These experiences make the disciples wiser and stronger. So it was with me. In my early years in the āśram, Amma used to tell me, "I will make you bold!" I had no idea what she meant.

Once, Amma called us to the swimming pool. She started pushing us into the pool. When it was my turn, I said, "Amma, I don't know how to swim."

"Aha!" she said, "You don't know how to swim?" Amma asked another brahmacāriṇī to bring a lifebelt, which she put around me. I was petrified. I looked at Amma, who was saying something to me, but I could not understand anything. The only thing I heard her say was, "I will make you bold!" Then she pushed me into the water! I heard Amma's voice telling me to hold on tightly to the lifebelt. She kept repeating it. Later, I started contemplating those words.

After this incident, I was posted to the Amrita Vidyalayam (school) in Thrissur. Within a few months, I found myself inundated by problems created by some parents, one of whom was a devotee of Amma. Things became so bad that I would go to bed feeling like I did not want to get up in the morning. I was in a constant state of anxiety.

Amma called me on the phone and said, "Don't give up. Never give up. Daughter, keep trying. Divine grace will crown your efforts with success!"

I recalled Amma's words in the swimming pool: to hold on tightly to the lifebelt. I felt that her words meant I should hold on to her tightly; she is the true lifesaver. By year end, the problems abated. Now, whenever I need a boost of self-confidence, I remind myself of Amma's words.

Amma usually visits Thrissur during the school vacation. When I heard that the devotee who had created problems in the school was coming for sēvā, I angrily proclaimed that if she came, I would not cooperate with her! Later, I forgot about my outburst.

After Amma's arrival, I went to sit near her during darśan. Turning to me, she asked, "Did you say that you wouldn't cooperate if that devotee came?" Sheepishly, I said yes. "I didn't know that you had become so bold!" Amma's tone was full of displeasure. Her words made me realize that I lacked discernment and humility.

Instead of giving undue importance to how we feel, a true disciple ought to do her duty and leave the rest to the Guru. I am reminded of an experience I had while studying for the final exams of my degree. Though I studied hard for the exams, I could not finish revising everything. I told my parents that I was not going to sit for the exams. They said, "Trust in Amma and do your best. Amma will take care of the rest."

The next day, my parents took me to the doctor, who diagnosed me with 'exam fever' and prescribed some pills. I had an early dinner, took the pill, and went to bed.

After the exams, we went to Kodungalloor to see Amma. I told her that my exams were over and that I did not do well. Amma asked, "You've already finished your exams, haven't you?"

I said, "Yes, Amma, but I did not do well."

She said, "It's enough that you sat for the exams."

Hearing this, my tension dissipated. When the results were released, I went to the college with my father. I was too scared to look at my results. My father informed me that I had passed with distinction! This was purely Amma's grace.

I did not know what to do next. As Amma was on the US tour, I could not ask her. But my mother had a dream in which Amma told her to send me for a Bachelor of Education (B.Ed.) degree program. I enrolled for the B.Ed. After I completed it, Amma sent me to Kodungalloor to teach in the Amrita Vidyalayam there. It was a residential school; it also proved to be a *Gurukula*[27] for me. It was where I learned the rudiments of being a teacher and about life in an āśram.

Over the years, Amma has taught me many spiritual lessons such as humility and surrender. Once, while looking for a suitable venue for a school program, I visited *Thekke Madhom*, a reputed institute of non-duality, in Thrissur. The center is believed to have been established by Padmapādācārya, one of the four disciples of Ādi Śaṅkarācārya, the foremost interpreter of non-duality. Padmapādācārya's original name was Sānandan. He had total faith in his Guru. Once, when Śaṅkarācārya called out to him, Sānandan, who was on the other side of the river, stepped into the river without any hesitation and started walking to the other side. With each step, a lotus (*padma*) appeared underneath his feet (*pāda*), supporting him. Thus, Sānandan came to be known as Padmapāda.

---

27 Literally, the clan (kula) of the preceptor (Guru); traditional school where students would stay with the Guru for the entire duration of their scriptural studies.

This incident reveals the disciple's complete surrender and the Guru's loving support. May all of us be able to develop this kind of devotion and faith in Amma.

25

Amrita Express

Br. Chandrasekhar

In July 2011, on the night of Guru Pūrṇimā, I boarded a train named Amrita Express. I was going to attend a meeting at the Ettimadai campus of Amrita University. The train arrived at Kayamkulam Junction shortly after midnight. After boarding the train, I found someone occupying my seat. When I harshly asked him to get up, he said that it was his seat. I went to the Ticket Collector (TC) to complain, only to discover that my ticket had been for the day before! The TC told me to alight at the next station. I did but rushed to the general compartment, which was so crowded that there was no place to sit.

As I stood there, perplexed, I began to recollect what had gone wrong. I had asked my travel agent to book the ticket for the night of July 10th. I should have told him to book it for the early morning of July 11th because Amrita Express arrives at Kayamkulam Junction at 12:15 a.m. I reflected on how harshly I had spoken to the passenger and TC. Amma thus revealed to me my lack of *śraddhā* (attentiveness), evident in my not checking the ticket.

Suddenly, someone asked me, "Why are you still carrying your bags? Why don't you put them down?" I was reminded of Amma's story about the passenger who bears his luggage on his head while traveling in a train, when it would have made no difference if he had put his luggage down, as it was the train bearing the weight of the passengers and their baggage. Similarly, we think we are doers and lug around the burden of 'I' and 'mine.'

Amma is an Amrita Express, carrying us to the abode of spirituality. All we need to do is to stay on board until we arrive at our destination: *mōkṣa* (spiritual liberation). Also, just as we would put our bags down after boarding a train, we must surrender the burden of our individuality after meeting Amma. When we do so, our individuality becomes one with the Supreme.

The journey, which moves along the tracks of Amma's love (Mā) and the light of her teachings (Ōm), is powered by our faith in Amma's *śakti* (divine power). The Amrita Express offers passengers a variety of spiritual practices to choose from—*japa* (repeated chanting of mantra), meditation and selfless service—to strengthen the mind so that it can better wage the inner Kurukṣētra War. Along the way, we might develop a bond with our co-passengers and possibly even quarrel with some of them, as we would with our brothers and sisters. This is meant only to smoothen our rough edges. If we are too abrasive, Amma, the resident surgeon, will step in to uproot our negative tendencies. Our journey is backed by God's insurance—*yōgakṣēmam vahāmyaham*—the assurance that He will safeguard what we have and provide what we lack. (*Bhagavad Gītā*, 9.22)

As we travel, we learn to become witnesses and not identify with passing sights. What we see when we look out of the window depends on where we are located. Similarly, our understanding of Amma is framed by our perspective. Some people call her a *mahātmā* (spiritually illumined soul). Others hail her as the Divine Mother. Some adore her as Kṛṣṇa, Kālī or Christ. Quite a few praise Amma as a great humanitarian leader or an environmentalist. Many regard her as their Guru. But regardless of how we see or label Amma, she remains *pūrṇa-brahma swarūpiṇī* (the complete manifestation of the Supreme), as mentioned in her *Aṣṭōttaram* (108 attributes, name 1).

Just as the sun does not require any credential to rise in the East, Amma does not need permission to fulfill her mission in life. Like Śrī Rāma and Śrī Kṛṣṇa before her, she is restoring the balance in creation by increasing the divine attributes and eliminating the evil tendencies in human beings. Amma is specifically reviving the quality of motherhood, which she says in present in both males and females, in the hearts of people all over the world. This is crucial for the survival of life on this planet. Vēdic seers beheld motherhood in all beings:

> *ya dēvī sarva bhūtēṣu mātṛ-rupēṇa samsthitā*
> The Goddess resides in all beings in the form of the Mother.

The Mother is everything. She is love, knowledge, energy and our very own. In India, the Mother is worshipped in six forms:

1. *Dēha-mātā*: our mother, who gave birth to us and nourishes us;
2. *Gō-mātā*: the cow, who nurtures us with her milk;
3. *Bhū-mātā*: Mother Earth, who sustains life and supports us;
4. *Gaṅgā-mātā*: the River Ganges, which irrigates the land, making it lush and green;

5. *Vēda-mātā*: the holy scriptures, which imparts spiritual wisdom;
6. *Jagan-mātā*: the Universal Mother, who has given birth to the whole of creation. The mother of mothers, she is present in every atom in this cosmos and in every cell of every being.

The harmony between man and nature has become disturbed. Amma says that Mother Nature is agitated because of human greed and ignorance. Natural calamities are increasing. Family ties are getting strained. The elderly are being consigned to old-age homes. There are more divorces, interpersonal conflicts and crimes in society. The presence of more women in the workforce is threatening the male ego. The children of working women are missing out on the presence of their mothers.

To combat this disharmony, Amma is restoring the dharma of motherhood through her healing touch. Over the last four-and-a-half decades, Amma has been working tirelessly to sow the seeds of love and compassion in our hearts. Amma says, "There are two kinds of poverty in the world—material poverty and the lack of compassion in human hearts." Through her words and deeds, she is inspiring us to love and serve others selflessly.

Amma is also reviving Sanātana Dharma.[28] Facets of this revival include her talks, bhajans, guided meditation and darśans. She is also initiating ever more people into the spiritual life by giving them mantras. Amma has established a number of Brahmasthānam Temples throughout India and one outside, and propagates the learning of Sanskrit and the scriptures. She has infused the four traditional *āśramas* (stages of life)—namely,

---

28 Literally 'Eternal Religion' or 'Eternal Way of Life,' the original and traditional name of Hinduism.

brahmacarya (celibate student life), *gārhasthya* (householder life), *vānaprastha* (life of seclusion), *and sannyāsa* (renunciation) — with the fresh air of spiritual wisdom. By conducting ceremonies such as the *annaprāśan* (first feeding), *vidyārambha* (initiation into learning), *vivāha* (marriage) and *śava samskāra* (funeral rites), Amma is upholding the importance of these age-old milestones in life.

By Amma's efforts, the *Lalitā Sahasranāma*, the 1,000 names of the Divine Mother, which used to be chanted by only an exclusive minority, is now being chanted daily by millions of people all over the world. Chanting the *Lalitā Sahasranāma* regularly helps to eliminate our demonic tendencies. The story of how Goddess Lalitā slew the demon Bhaṇḍāsura is narrated in the *Lalitōpakhyāna* of the *Brahmāṇḍa Purāṇa*. Bhaṇḍāsura and his brothers were terrorizing the three worlds by entering the bodies and minds of divine beings, humans and other beings, and spread their contagion everywhere, much like the coronavirus. All beings lost interest in life. They became stone-like and stopped loving or helping each other. Creation came to a grinding halt.

The gods beseeched the Divine Mother for help. She manifested as Goddess Lalitā, holding four weapons: a sugarcane bow representing the mind; arrows of flowers representing sense perceptions; the rope of love; and the goad of anger. The Goddess assumed the form of anger and created an army of yōginīs. The battle between Bhaṇḍāsura and Dēvī was a clash between negative and positive energies. Bhaṇḍāsura unleashed negative energies like forgetfulness, ignorance, hurdles, heresy, toxicity, perversion, diseases and cruelty, which Dēvī countered with positive energies such as knowledge, concentration, fearlessness and longevity.

Amma has all the attributes of Goddess Lalitā. Her smile, words, looks and touch are beautiful and gentle. She binds us with the rope of love so that we will not fall into the trap of *Māyā*, cosmic delusion. When Amma guides us during meditation, she sounds the gong to arrest the distracted mind. She punctures our inflated egos and sets us back on the path of dharma by a show of anger. The arrows Amma shoots are the white flowers of peace. Since 2017, when she started the White Flower meditation, she has been asking us to shower the flowers of peace on all, all over the world, thus helping us neutralize the negative tendencies of our own mind and that of the world with vibes of goodwill. She encourages scriptural study, infuses strength in the mind, and empowers us to eradicate the Bhaṇḍāsura within ourselves. There is no firewall as secure as prayer to protect us from the virus of negativity.

Singing the glories of God is an important devotional practice. One day, while sitting near Amma, I heard someone singing stories about Amma in Malayāḷam. Hearing this, I felt inspired to write a *Bhāgavatam* (sacred narrative) about Amma, one describing her *līlās* (divine play), in Telugu. Later, the singer told me that singing Amma's glories in various places had cured his disease. Amma asked me, "Son, did you write that bhajan '*Adi sṛṣṭi lōpamā?*' Amma likes it; many other people also love it!" She then gave me the cup of water from which she had been sipping. I took this as a sign from Amma to proceed with my desire to compose the *Amma Bhāgavatam*.

Over the next 40 days, wonderful and simple Telugu verses began to take form. I wrote around 200 verses describing

Amma's early life, and wrote up to her first Kṛṣṇa Bhāva darśan. Then, I encountered many obstacles and could not write another line, even though I tried.

During this time, a brahmacārī told Amma that I was attempting to write her *Bhāgavatam*. After six months, when I went for my room darśan, the first question Amma asked me was, "Are you writing Amma's *Bhāgavatam*? Can you do it?"

I replied that I could, with her grace, and that I had already written 200 verses to date. She said I should first read the *Śrīmad Bhāgavatam* and her biography. Hearing this, I felt humbled. I realized that I was not qualified for such a sacred undertaking, for which one must have tremendous inner purity.

I then told Amma about my diabetes and sought her permission to go for naturopathy treatment. She agreed. She then told me to open my mouth. She put some prasād into it.

As advised, I read Amma's biography twice and listened to the recitation of the *Śrīmad Bhāgavatam* a few times. I was still not able to write even one more verse. But by her grace, I started writing articles about her for Telugu *Matruvani*. These were eventually compiled and published as a book.

These efforts produced another kind of miracle: my diabetes came under control without my taking any medicine! For the last five years, I have not been taking any medication. I stopped eating sweets and have lost about 25 kilograms by reducing my carbohydrate intake substantially and by eating more fruits and vegetables. I also practice haṭha yōga and walk 30 minutes daily. Both my energy and awareness levels have increased.

My case amazed the medical fraternity, which still finds it hard to believe that my diabetes has come under control without any medication. It is my faith that my modest attempts at writing Amma's *Bhāgavatam* helped to bring the disease under control.

I have come to realize that whether composing Telugu bhajans, authoring books on Amma and Indian culture, teaching in the college, doing sēvā related to Amma's programs, or liaising with government officials on matters pertaining to āśram institutions, my planning never works. Only when I surrender my will and allow Amma's will to prevail do my efforts succeed. I have also realized that I can put in effort only because of her grace. It is Amma's divine will that powers our journey on Amrita Express.

Glossary

adharma: unrighteousness; deviation from natural harmony.
Ādi Śaṅkarācārya: saint revered as a Guru and chief proponent of the Advaita (non-dual) philosophy.
Advaita: not two; non-dual; philosophy that holds that the *jīva* (individual soul) and *jagat* (universe) are essentially one with Brahman, the supreme reality.
ahimsā: *non-violence.*
AIMS Hospital: Amrita Institute of Medical Sciences, a super-specialty hospital in Kochi, Kerala.
ajñāna: ignorance (of the spiritual truth); an ***ajñānī*** is one who is ignorant.
Amala Bharatam Campaign: a cleaning campaign aimed at cleaning India's public places and national highways, and raising public awareness about cleanliness and hygiene; Amma launched this campaign on September 27th, 2010, during her 57th birthday celebrations.
Amma: 'mother' in Malayāḷam and various other Indian languages.
Amrita Kuṭumbam: literally, 'Amrita family.' It refers to a regular gathering of devotees in a locality for the purpose of spiritual practices such as arcana, meditation and bhajans.
Amrita Vidyalayam: a national network of schools managed by the Mata Amritanandamayi Math and offering value-based education at the primary and secondary levels.

Amrita Vishwa Vidyapeetham: a private, accredited, multi-campus, multidisciplinary university, currently ranked among the best in India.

Amṛtadhāra: literally, a 'flow of nectar.' A poetic rendition of Amma's teachings by Swāmī Turīyamṛtānanda Puri, one of Amma's senior monastic disciples.

Amṛtapuri: The international headquarters of Mata Amritanandamayi Math, located at Amma's birthplace in Kerala, India.

arcana: chanting of the 108 or 1,000 names of a particular deity (e.g. *'Lalita Sahasranāma'*).

Arjuna: great archer and one of the heroes of the *Mahābhārata*. It is Arjuna whom Kṛṣṇa addresses in the *Bhagavad Gītā*.

artha: goal, wealth, substance; one of the four *puruṣārthas* (goals of human endeavor).

āśram: monastery. Amma defines it as a compound: *'ā'* — 'that' and *'śramam'* — 'effort' (toward Self-realization).

āśrama: one of the four stages of life in traditional India; they include *brahmacarya* (celibate student life), *gārhasthya* (householder life), *vānaprastha* (retired life dedicated to spiritual practices) and *sannyāsa* (life of complete renunciation); also, a halting place or hermitage.

Aṣṭōttaram: litany of 108 attributes of a deity, divine incarnation or saint; short form of *aṣṭōttara-śatam* (108) or *aṣṭōttara-śata-nāmāvali* (108 names).

ātmā: Self or soul.

avadhūta: an enlightened person whose behavior is often eccentric and at odds with social norms.

avatār: from Sanskrit root *'ava-tarati'* — 'to come down.' Incarnation of the Divine.

AYUDH: 'Amrita Yuva Dharmadhara,' the youth wing of the Mata Amritanandamayi Math.

Bhagavad Gītā: 'Song of the Lord,' it consists of 18 chapters of verses in which Lord Kṛṣṇa counsels Arjuna. The advice is given on the battlefield of Kurukṣētra, just before the righteous Pāṇḍavas fight the unrighteous Kauravas. It is a practical guide to overcoming crises in one's personal or social life and is the essence of Vēdic wisdom.
bhajan: devotional song or hymn in praise of God.
bhakti: devotion for God.
Bhārat: India.
Bhāva: divine mood or attitude.
Bhīṣma: patriarch of the Pāṇḍava and Kaurava clan. Though he fought on the side of the Kauravas during the Mahābhārata War, he championed dharma and was sympathetic to the righteous Pāṇḍavas.
Brahma: Lord of Creation in the Hindu Trinity.
brahmacāri: celibate male disciple who practices spiritual disciplines under a Guru's guidance; '***brahmacāriṇī***' is the female equivalent.
brahmacarya: celibacy; see *āśrama*. Brahma also means Vēda. So, brahmacarya is the stage of life in which one pursues the study of the Vēdas with self-discipline under the guidance of an *ācārya* (teacher).
Brahman: ultimate truth beyond any attributes; the supreme reality underlying all life; the divine ground of existence.
Brahmasthānam: 'abode of Brahman.' The name of the temples Amma consecrated in various parts of India and in Mauritius.

The temple shrine features a unique four-faced idol that symbolizes the unity behind the diversity of divine forms.
Brāhmin: member of the priestly caste, whose duty it is to study and teach the Vēdas.
Buddha: from '*budh,*' meaning 'to wake up;' also, a reference to Sage Gautama Buddha, a spiritual master whose teachings form the foundation of Buddhism.

caitanya: consciousness.

dakṣiṇa: Honorarium given to the Guru as a token of the disciple's gratitude and appreciation.
Dakṣiṇamūrti: An aspect of Lord Śiva, the Destroyer in the Hindu Trinity. Also considered the first Guru.
Damayanti-amma: Amma's mother.
darśan: audience with a holy person or a vision of the Divine. Amma's signature darśan is a hug.
Daśaratha: Father of Rāma and king of Kōśala.
Dēvī Bhāva: 'the divine mood of Dēvī;' occasion when Amma reveals her oneness with the Divine Mother.
Dēvī: Goddess / Divine Mother.
dharma: 'that which upholds (creation).' Generally refers to the harmony of the universe, a righteous code of conduct, sacred duty or eternal law.
dīkṣā: initiation into the vows of *brahmacarya* or *sannyāsa* or any form of spiritual discipline such as *japa* (repeated chanting of a mantra) and *dhyāna* (meditation).
Draupadī: main female protagonist of the *Mahābhārata* and common consort of the Pāṇḍava brothers.
Durvāsa: a legendary *ṛṣi* known for his flaming temper.

Dwāpara Yuga: see *yuga.*

gōpī: milk maiden from Vṛndāvan. The gōpīs were known for their ardent devotion to Lord Kṛṣṇa. Their devotion exemplifies the most intense love for God.
gṛhastha: householder; member of the second of four *āśramas* (stages of life), which include *brahmacarya* (celibate student life), *gārhasthya* (married householder life), *vānaprastha* (life of retirement and contemplation) and *sannyāsa.*
guṇa: one of three types of qualities, *viz.* sattva, rajas and tamas. Human beings express a combination of these qualities. Sāttvic qualities are associated with calmness and wisdom, rajasic qualities with activity and restlessness, and tāmasic qualities with dullness or apathy.
Guru: spiritual teacher.
Gurukula: literally, the clan (*kula*) of the preceptor (*Guru*); traditional school where students would stay with the Guru for the entire duration of their scriptural studies.
Guruvāyūrappan: a form of Lord Vishnu, worshipped mainly in Kerala.

hōma: ancient Vēdic fire ritual in which oblations are offered to the gods by offering ghee into a consecrated fire; a *dēva-yajña*, one of the five daily *yajñas* to be performed by a Brahmin.

itihāsa: 'traditional account of past events.' Generally used to refer to the *Rāmāyaṇa* and the *Mahābhārata.*

japa: repeated chanting of a mantra.
-jī: an honorific suffixed to names or titles to show respect.

jīva: individual self or soul.
jñāna: knowledge of the Truth. A ***jñānī*** is one who knows the Truth.

Kaikēyī: second wife of Daśaratha and mother of Bharata (in the *Rāmāyaṇa*).
kaḷari: temple where Amma used to hold Kṛṣṇa Bhāva and Dēvī Bhāva darśans.
Kali Yuga: see *yuga*.
Kāḷī: Goddess of fearsome aspect; depicted as dark, wearing a garland of skulls, and a girdle of human hands; feminine of Kāla (time).
kāma: desire.
kaññi: rice gruel.
karma: action; mental, verbal and physical activity; chain of effects produced by our actions.
karma yōga: the way of action, the path of selfless service.
Kauravas: the 101 children of King Dhṛtarāṣṭra and Queen Gāndhārī, of whom the unrighteous Duryōdhana was the eldest. The Kauravas were the enemies of their cousins, the virtuous Pāṇḍavas, whom they fought against in the Mahābhārata War.
Kṛṣṇa Bhāva: 'the divine mood of Kṛṣṇa,' occasion when Amma reveals her oneness with Lord Kṛṣṇa.
Kṛṣṇa: from '*kṛṣ*,' meaning 'to draw to oneself' or 'to remove sin;' principal incarnation of Lord Viṣṇu. He was born into a royal family but raised by foster parents, and lived as a cowherd boy in Vṛndāvan, where he was loved and worshipped by his devoted companions, the *gōpīs* (milkmaids) and *gōpas* (cowherd boys). Kṛṣṇa later established the city of Dwāraka. He was a friend and advisor to his cousins, the Pāṇḍavas, especially Arjuna, whom

he served as charioteer during the Mahābhārata War, and to whom he revealed his teachings as the *Bhagavad Gītā.*
Kṣatriya: ruler or warrior; one of the four *varṇas* (social order) of ancient Hindu society.
kṣētra: literally, 'field.' In the 13th chapter of the *Bhagavad Gītā*, the term refers to the perishable body.
kṣētrajña: literally, 'knower of the field.' In the 13th chapter of the *Bhagavad Gītā*, the term refers to the imperishable knower of the body, i.e. the indwelling Self.
Kurukṣētra: battlefield where the war between the Pāṇḍavas and Kauravas was fought; also, a metaphor for the conflict between good and evil.

Lalitā Sahasranāma: 1,000 names of Śrī Lalita Dēvī, a form of the Goddess.
līlā: divine play.

Mahābhārata: ancient Indian epic that Sage Vyāsa composed, depicting the war between the righteous Pāṇḍavas and the unrighteous Kauravas.
mahātmā: 'great soul;' term used to describe one who has attained spiritual realization.
Malayāḷam: language spoken in the Indian state of Kerala.
mānasa pūjā: worship done mentally.
mantra: a sound, syllable, word or words of spiritual content. According to Vēdic commentators, mantras are revelations of ṛṣis arising from deep contemplation.
Mā-Ōm meditation: a meditation technique formulated by Amma, one that involves synchronizing the silent intonation of the syllables 'Mā' and 'Ōm' with the inhalation and exhalation.

Matruvani: 'Voice of the Mother.' The āśram's flagship publication dedicated to disseminating Amma's teachings and chronicling her divine mission. It is currently published in 17 languages (including nine Indian languages).

Māyā: cosmic delusion, personified as a temptress. Illusion; appearance, as contrasted with reality; the creative power of the Lord.

mōkṣa: spiritual liberation, i.e. release from the cycle of births and deaths.

Nārada: a ṛṣi or sage, mind-born son of Brahma, and *loka-Guru* (world teacher). He inspired Vālmīki to compose the *Rāmāyaṇa*. In the *Mahābhārata*, he visited the Pāṇḍavas a number of times to advise them on the right course of action. He also tried to broker peace between the Pāṇḍavas and Kauravas but failed.

Ōm (Aum): primordial sound in the universe; the seed of creation. The cosmic sound, which can be heard in deep meditation; the Holy Word, taught in the Upaniṣads, which signifies Brahman, the divine ground of existence.

Ōṇam: Kerala's biggest festival, occurring in the month of *Ciṅṅam* (August – September).

Ōṭṭūr Uṇṇi Nanpūtirippāḍ: composer of Amma's ***Aṣṭōttaram***.

pañca mahāyajñas: five great sacrifices to be performed daily by householders, viz. *Brahma-yajña* (studying / teaching the Vēdas); the *tarpaṇa* (offering libations of water to deceased ancestors) is *Pitṛ-yajña*; the hōma is *Dēva-yajña* (offerings to the gods); the *bali* (offering a portion of the daily meal of rice, grain, ghee, etc. to all creatures) is *Bhūta-yajña*; and the honoring of guests is *Nṛ-yajña*.

Pāṇḍavas: five sons of King Pāṇḍu, and cousins of Kṛṣṇa.
paradharma: duty of others, as opposed to *swadharma.*
pāyasam: pudding.
prakṛti: nature or matter; the active principle of creation, as opposed to *puruṣa*, the passive principle.
prārabdha: also known as *prārabdha karma*; refers to the part of our past karma that is the cause of our present birth.
prasād: blessed offering or gift from a holy person or temple, often in the form of food.
prasāda buddhi: the attitude of seeing everything one receives as a gift from God.
pūjā: ritualistic or ceremonial worship.
Purāṇas: compendium of stories, including the biographies and stories of gods, saints, kings and great people; allegories and chronicles of great historical events that aim to make the teachings of the Vēdas simple and available to all.
Puruṣa: pure consciousness, as opposed to *prakṛti*; the Supreme.
puruṣārtha: the four ultimate goals of human life, namely *dharma* (righteousness), *artha* (material wealth), *kāma* (desire) and *mōkṣa* (spiritual liberation).

Rādhā: one of the *gōpīs* (milkmaids) of Vṛndāvan, often lauded for her pure and selfless devotion to Lord Kṛṣṇa.
rajas: see *guṇa.*
Rāma: divine hero of the *Rāmāyaṇa.* An incarnation of Lord Viṣṇu, he is considered the ideal man of *dharma* and virtue. *'Ram'* means 'to revel;' one who revels in himself; the principle of joy within; one who gladdens the hearts of others.
Rāmakṛṣṇa Paramahamsa: spiritual master (1836 – 1886) from West Bengal, hailed as the apostle of religious harmony.

He generated a spiritual renaissance that continues to touch the lives of millions.
Ramaṇa Maharṣi: spiritual master (1879 – 1950) who lived in Tiruvannamalai, Tamil Nadu. He recommended Self-inquiry as the path to Liberation, though he approved of a variety of paths and spiritual practices.
Rāmāyaṇa: 24,000-verse epic poem on the life and times of Rāma.
Rāvaṇa: powerful demon king. Viṣṇu incarnated as Lord Rāma to kill him and thereby restore harmony to the world.
ṛṣi: spiritually enlightened being and seer to whom mantras and the secrets of the universe were revealed in deep meditation.

sādhana: regimen of disciplined and dedicated spiritual practice that leads to the supreme goal of Self-realization.
samādhi: literally, 'cessation of all mental movements;' oneness with God; a transcendental state in which one loses all sense of individual identity; union with absolute reality; a state of intense concentration in which consciousness is completely unified.
samatva: even-mindedness or equanimity.
samsāra: cycle of births and deaths; the world of flux; the wheel of birth, decay, death and rebirth.
samskāra: a personality trait conditioned over many lives or one life: a mental and behavioral pattern; a latency or tendency within the mind which will manifest itself if given the proper environment or stimulus.
Sanātana Dharma: literally, 'Eternal Religion' or 'Eternal Way of Life,' the original and traditional name of Hinduism.
saṅkalpa: divine resolve, usually used in association with *mahātmās*.

sannyāsī: monk who has taken formal vows of renunciation (*sannyāsa*); traditionally wears an ocher-colored robe, representing the burning away of all desires. The female equivalent is ***sannyāsinī.***

satsaṅg: communion with the Supreme Truth. Also, being in the company of *mahātmās*, studying the scriptures, and listening to the enlightening talks of a mahātmā; a meeting of people to listen to and/or discuss spiritual matters; a spiritual discourse.

sattva: see *guṇa.*

Satya Yuga: see *yuga.*

sēvā: selfless service, the results of which are dedicated to God.

Śiva: worshipped as the first and the foremost in the lineage of Gurus, and as the formless substratum of the universe in relationship to Śakti. The Lord of Destruction in the Hindu Trinity.

Śiva-linga: literally, 'emblem of Shiva.' An abstract representation of the beginningless and endless nature of the Divine.

Sītā: Rāma's consort. In India, she is considered to be the ideal of womanhood.

śraddhā: attentiveness; faith.

Śrīmad Bhāgavatam: also known as *Bhāgavatam*, a Sanskrit composition that upholds devotion to Lord Viṣṇu, the Sustainer in the Hindu Trinity. It is one of the 18 Purāṇas. It narrates the life, pastimes and teachings of various incarnations of Viṣṇu, chiefly that of Lord Kṛṣṇa.

sthita-prajña: person of 'steady wisdom,' who has renounced all desires and is established in the Self.

Śūdra: service providers; one of the four *varṇas* (social order) of ancient Hindu society.

Suguṇānandan-acchan: Amma's father.

swadharma: personal dharma or one's own duties; opposed to *paradharma.*

swādhyāya: 'self-study;' recitation of the Vēdas and other sacred texts.

Swāmī Vivēkānanda: chief disciple (1863 - 1902) of Śrī Rāmakṛṣṇa Paramahamsa, a pioneer in introducing Hindu philosophy to the West, and founder of the Ramakrishna Math and Ramakrishna Mission.

Swāmī: title of one who has taken the vow of *sannyāsa* (see *sannyāsī*); **Swāminī** is the female equivalent.

tamas: see *guṇa.*

tapas: austerities, penance.

Trēta Yuga: see *yuga.*

Uddhava: character in the *Mahābhārata* and the *Bhāgavata Purāṇa*; friend of and adviser to Lord Kṛṣṇa.

Upaniṣad: portions of the Vēdas dealing with Self-knowledge.

vairāgya: dispassion.

Vaiśya: farmers and traders; one of the four *varṇas* (social order) of ancient Hindu society.

Vallikavu: place where the Amṛtapuri Āśram is located.

Vālmīki: sage and author of the *Rāmāyaṇa.*

vānaprastha: 'forest life;' a reference to the retired life dedicated to spiritual practices; the third of the four stages of life (see *āśrama*).

varṇa: the four-fold social order of ancient Indian society that includes the Brāhmins, Kṣatriyas, Vaiśyas and Śūdras.

vāsanā: latent tendency or subtle desire that manifests as thought, motive and action; subconscious impression gained from experience.

vasudhaiva kuṭumbakam: 'the world is one family.'

Vēdānta: 'the end of the Vēdas.' It refers to the Upaniṣads, which deal with the subject of Brahman, the supreme truth, and the path to realize that Truth; a Vēdāntin is a follower of Vēdānta.

Vēdas: most ancient of all scriptures, originating from God, the Vēdas were not composed by any human author but were 'revealed' in deep meditation to the ancient seers. These sagely revelations came to be known as the Vēdas, of which there are four: *Ṛk*, *Yajus*, *Sāma* and *Atharva.*

Viṣṇu: Lord of Sustenance in the Hindu Trinity.

Viṣu: popular Hindu festival celebrated in Kerala and which coincides with the spring equinox.

viśwās: faith

vivēka: discernment, especially between the ephemeral and eternal.

Vṛndāvan: pilgrimage destination in present-day Uttar Pradesh, India, associated with the childhood days and youth of Lord Kṛṣṇa.

Vyāsa: literally 'compiler.' The name given to Sage Kṛṣṇa Dvaipāyana, who compiled the Vēdas. He is also the chronicler of the *Mahābhārata* and a character in it, and author of the 18 Purāṇas and the *Brahma-Sūtras.*

yajña: form of ritual worship in which oblations are offered into a fire according to scriptural injunctions, while sacred mantras are chanted.

yōga: 'to unite.' Union with the Supreme Being. A broad term, it also refers to the various methods of practices through which one can attain oneness with the Divine. A path that leads to Self-realization.

Yudhiṣṭhira: the eldest of the righteous Pāṇḍava brothers who waged war against the Kauravas, their unrighteous cousins, in the *Mahābhārata*.

yuga: according to the Hindu worldview, the universe (from origin to dissolution) passes through a cycle made up of four yugas or ages. The first is *Kṛta Yuga*, during which dharma reigns in society. Each succeeding age sees the progressive decline of dharma. The second age is known as *Trēta Yuga*, the third is *Dwāpara Yuga*, and the fourth and present epoch is known as *Kali Yuga*.

Pronunciation Guide

Vowels can be short or long:
a – as 'u' in but; ā – as 'a' in far
e – as 'a' in may; ē – as 'a' in name
i – as 'i' in pin; ī – as 'ee' in meet
o – as in oh; ō – as 'o' in mole
u – as 'u' in push; ū – as 'oo' in hoot

ṛ – as ri in crisp
ḥ – pronounce 'aḥ' like 'aha,' 'iḥ' like 'ihi,' and 'uḥ' like 'uhu.'

Some consonants are aspirated (e.g. kh); others are not (e.g. k). The examples given below are only approximate:
k – as 'k' in 'kite;' kh – as 'ckh' in 'Eckhart'
g – as 'g' in 'give;' gh – as 'g-h' in 'dig-hard'
c – as 'c' in 'cello;' ch – as 'ch-h' in 'staunch-heart'
j – as 'j' in 'joy;' jh – as 'dgeh' in 'hedgehog'
p – as 'p' in 'pine;' ph – as 'ph' in 'up-hill'
b – as 'b' in 'bird;' bh – as 'bh' in 'rub-hard'

r – as 'r' in ride
ñ – as 'ny' in 'canyon;' ṅ – as 'ng' in 'sing'

The letters ḍ, ṭ, ṇ are pronounced with the tip of the tongue against the hard palate, the others with the tip against the teeth.
ṭ – as 't' in 'tub;' ṭh – as 'th' in 'lighthouse'
ḍ – as 'd' in 'dove;' ḍh – as 'dh' in 'red-hot'
ṇ – as 'n' in 'naught'
ḷ – as 'l' in 'revelry'
ṣ – as 'sh' in 'shine;' ś – as 's' in German 'sprechen'

With double consonants the sound is pronounced twice:
cc – as 'tc' in 'hot chip'
jj – as 'dj' in 'red jet'

Acknowledgments

I express my heartfelt gratitude to Rosario (Rose) Kerekes for spearheading the editing of this compilation of talks. I also benefited from the assistance and guidance of an able team that includes Sharanya Muthupalani, Veena O'Sullivan, Rta Sutcliffe, Dayakaran Hirtenstein and Savitri Bess.

My heartfelt thanks also to Brī. Amṛta Caitanyā, who painstakingly went through the text and added diacritical marks. Swāmī Jñānāmṛtānanda reviewed both the text and layout, and offered invaluable suggestions.

I thank them all.

Br. Mādhavāmṛta Caitanya

www.ingramcontent.com/pod-product-compliance
Lightning Source LLC
LaVergne TN
LVHW051542080426
835510LV00020B/2817